So You Want to Do Ministry

John Walsh, M.M.
and
James DiGiacomo, S.J.

Sheed & Ward

Sheed and Ward™ is a service of National Catholic Reporter Publish-
ing, Inc.

Library of Congress Catalog Card Number: 85-63107

ISBN: 0-934134-77-4

Published by:

Sheed and Ward
115 E. Armour Blvd. P.O. Box 414292
Kansas City, MO 64141-0281

To order, call: (800)821-7926

CONTENTS

Part One: Diagnosis

Part Two: Prescription

Part One: Diagnosis

1
THE PRESENT RELIGIOUS CRISIS

The Best of Times, the Worst of Times

In the opening scene of the Broadway hit, *The Music Man*, a group of travelling salesmen are riding on a train travelling through the midwest and discussing the prospects of a new drummer whose mercantile star seems to be on the rise. A lively debate ensues, only to grind to a halt at the same time as the train, as a veteran intones the ultimate putdown: "But he doesn't know the territory!"

Anyone who wants to exercise Christian ministry in a pastorally effective way had better know the territory. Ice cubes don't sell among the Eskimoes, and it's hard to move fur coats in Hawaii. Preaching the Gospel is not exactly the same as selling, but it's not totally different, either. A message of salvation may sound like the best news of the year, or like the latest kind of snake oil. It depends not only on the preacher but also on the preachees. Who are these people? What are they looking for? What gets them up in the morning? What turns them on and off? What gives meaning to their lives, purpose to their struggles?

Foreign missionaries routinely ask themselves these questions when they are assigned to some distant land. They wouldn't think of going without gaining as thorough a knowledge as possible of the country — its people, culture, and language; the social, economic, and political landscape. They know that all these elements will affect the way the Gospel is heard and received in this land, by these people, at this moment in history. Those who stay in the United States and try to do ministry in the last years of the twentieth century must do no less. That is the thesis of this book.

Throughout these chapters, we will be analyzing the mentality of people inside and outside the church at least to the extent of having their names registered on the roles. We are writing at the end of two decades of extraordinary change, in the midst of developments that have profoundly altered the religious landscape. Many of the old landmarks are gone, and with them many of the people who once called the church their spiritual home. New patterns and styles of ministry have emerged to mixed reviews. Much of the dust has cleared since the winds of postconciliar change swept through the household of the faith, and it is now possible to get a reading of our present position and to plot a course for the future.

A broad overview of the American church as it enters the last decades of the twentieth century reveals both bad news and good news. Indeed, it is no exaggeration to say that the last third of this century has been the best of times and the worst of times.

First, the bad news. After the Second Vatican Council, a loss of symbols and traditional devotions undermined Catholics' sense of belonging and brought on, for many, an acute crisis of identity. A liturgical tradition, together with a rich patrimony of sacred music, virtually disappeared. Polarization and alienation took their toll, most visibly in the many empty pews at what used to be standing-room-only Sunday Masses. A mass exodus from the priesthood and from religious life severely diminished the ranks of full-time, dedicated professionals. Schools closed at an alarming rate. Changing patterns of religious education were not uniformly successful, and by the end of the seventies charges of religious illiteracy spawned a back-to-basics movement. A startling decline in the reception of the sacrament of Penance, despite an improved ritual, was only the tip of the iceberg, as moral theology underwent unsettling changes and radically affected the experience of sin, guilt and repentance. A crisis of authority, climaxing in the massive rejection, by laity and many clergy, of papal teaching on birth control, created deep division within the church. Many of the antagonists in religious controversies, exhausted by a dialogue of the deaf, became casualties of disillusion and apathy, and dropped out. An uneasy malaise ensued and still lies just below the surface of Catholic communities and drains their energies. The monolithic unity of the preconciliar church, with all the institutional strength of its united front, has disappeared. Many fear that commitment and dedication are on the way out, too, and wonder: has the church lost its soul?

And yet this is not the whole story. Consider the good things that have happened in this same turbulent period. The liturgical renewal has survived the inevitable growing pains and has seen a genuine revitalization of worship not only in the celebration of Eucharist but also in the administration of the sacraments. Movements such as charismatics, prayer groups, marriage encounter, cursillo and new forms of youth retreats are impressive signs of vitality. If there are fewer people in church on Sunday, significant numbers are more involved and serious about what they are doing, as the quality of religious experience becomes, for many, just as important as its regularity. The drop in vocations to clerical and religious life has been offset by a coming of age of the laity who are no longer content with being "Father's helpers"; as a result, clerical domination of the life of the church has been eroded though far from eliminated. Religious education has become a much more sophisticated enterprise as help has come from the behavioral sciences, especially developmental psychology. We understand better now how young people grow and learn and assimilate religious and moral perspectives; and adult religious education is valued at least in theory if not yet in practice. Youth ministry is an old field with a new agenda and a new corps of professionals. The crisis of confidence in church authority has helped produce in many Catholics a new level of maturity in the responsible exercise of conscience. A genuine commitment to justice and peace in the hierarchy as well as in many of the laity and lower clergy has broken through some of the churchy parochialism that periodically bedevils ecclesiastical institutions.

All this adds up to a richness and diversity in church life that has its shortcomings and ambiguities but gives promise of a rich harvest, if the laborers in the vineyard know what they are about. This book offers help to the laborers. We offer a vision, a perspective, a program and an array of strategies aimed at realizing the enormous potential for religious growth in the present situation.

How should we respond to this moment? What are the resources and skills required for effective ministry? The first place to look is not Scripture or tradition or theology. To do ministry, one obviously needs grounding and development in those areas, as well as a commitment to prayer and personal spiritual growth. But as fundamental as these are, they will not, all by themselves, yield an answer to the questions we are asking. Rather, we must explore what is happening to the people we wish to serve. The late Karl Rahner, a man not given to hyperbole, said that the church is going through the most radical shift it has experienced since 50 A.D. Even our cursory description of the religious scene makes it clear that we are dealing with a new kind of hearer. There *is* something new under the sun, and its name is people. They have different expectations, different felt needs. To serve them, more is required than a rearranging of church furniture. A new approach is called for, one that responds to the real needs of real people, not the needs we would like them to have or that we think they should have. We must answer the questions they are asking, not necessarily the ones on our minds. In some cases, we will even have to help them ask new questions. And sometimes we may have to put new questions to ourselves.

The good things that have happened since the Council were

possible because people listened to one another. They took one another seriously and recognized that they had changed. When people talk about the changes in the church, they tend to think of *things* that have been altered — language, structures, practices, rituals. What they often fail to perceive is that *people* usually change first, then their practices. When traditional modes of religious expression no longer fulfilled their purpose, they were either modified or discarded. A new kind of church emerged in the last decades of this century because a new kind of person had already appeared on the scene.

What happened? The people that make up the church have changed, and so have their religious expectations and practices. Inevitably, the institution itself has been transformed. For centuries, it had been like the Rock of Gibraltar — static, strong, secure, safe — with styles of ministry and spirituality to match. Now, after two decades of upheaval, a few church members still feel that the institution has changed too much, and feel disoriented and betrayed. For many more, the institution has not changed nearly enough, and these are frustrated and impatient. And there are great numbers who are simply losing interest and wandering off, because they feel ignored or misunderstood by ministers who are unable to comprehend their needs or respond to them.

Unless we understand what is happening to people (including ourselves!), much of our efforts in spirituality and ministry will go to waste. Neglect to do this in these changing times, and confusion may reign in your spiritual life. Neglect to do this, and no matter how hard you work at ministry, your efforts will get only twenty cents on the dollar.

So let us begin to examine, and take seriously, what is happening to the people we wish to serve.

2
WHERE ARE WE COMING FROM?

No Longer the Way We Were

The movement that has affected the church in our time has been nothing less than a quantum leap — the first that Christ's followers have experienced in centuries. A quantum leap is a major change, a radical transformation. It is not to be confused with a cosmetic change, a mere rearrangement of items on the surface without deep-seated alteration.

A quantum leap occurs in rapid fashion with great force. For a very long time (in this case, centuries) nothing much apparently happens. Then the critical point is reached and quantum change is under way, catching those involved unaware and unprepared. Pull back the trigger on a rifle ninety-nine percent of the way, and nothing happens. Pull it one more millimeter and there is an explosion, sending the bullet on its way.

When the critical point of a quantum leap is reached, it begets crisis. The Japanese have an interesting word for this: *kiki*. It is best translated "dangerous opportunity." Fraught with danger, but with enormous potential for good. Our generation is faced with a great responsibility — to bring the second millenium of Christianity to completion. If we freeze in front of the all too apparent dangers and try to reduce quantum leap to cosmetic change, we fail. And, paradoxically, we bring on even greater dangers. But if we rise to the challenge presented to us, the possibilities are limitless. Few generations in the religious history of humanity have received an opportunity like the one now facing us.

But what is happening at the core of today's events? In what does the quantum leap of Christianity consist? It is a deepseated change in the people of God who comprise the church. There is a radical change in the way people *appropriate* or *take possession of* their faith. It extends to how they interpret the meaning of life (beliefs) to how they live this life (actions). And with this change in appropriation of faith there comes a change in all aspects of life, even if it is not immediately apparent.

This shift in appropriation of religious values can best be described in terms of movement from

<u>*Traditional*</u>
> to
> > <u>*Transitional*</u> (One model)
> > > to
> > > > <u>*Integrated*</u> (Many models)

Traditional

At this level of faith-appropriation one is indoctrinated into the teachings of the faith. This is not to suggest brainwashing (although this is possible), so let us write the word as "in-doc-trination." One is introduced into the stories of the tribe. These are the group's most precious treasures which are passed on to each generation: "This is how we interpret life; this is how we try to live." Since most people first learn their religion as children, this is an appropriate way to begin, for children simply accept uncritically what their elders teach them.

The person is then socialized into this faith and carried along by a support parade (parish, school, ethnic neighborhood, religious community). In fact, the word "parade" is a good capsule description of traditional appropriation.

Let us consider the characteristics of a parade:

1) union by uniformity,

2) by following significant others

3) in a non-judgmental way.

Suppose you were asked to sum up Christianity in one word. No fair using the word "Christ," since that is already contained in the word to be defined. Suppose someone said to you, "What are you Christians about? What are you trying to do? What do you see as the meaning, the fulfillment of life?" Limited to one word, a good choice might be *union*. We are seeking union with Christ and with one another. Now this union is attained, at the traditional level of appropriation, by uniformity. If we all basically think alike, theologize alike, pray alike, and have a similar life style, then union will be attained. But don't confuse means and ends. Uniformity is only the means, union is the end. Unfortunately, many people feel that uniformity is the *only* means for attaining the purpose of Christianity. So when someone suggests that in these changing times there could be other and perhaps better ways of attaining union, he or she is often accused of attacking Christianity itself and its servant, church.

The second characteristic of this level of appropriation is to follow significant others. They may be parent, brother, sister, priest, teacher, political authority, military authority, etc.

These significant others are followed for the most part in a non-judgmental way. One does not question the direction the parade called Christianity or church is going in (its immediate objectives) or the beat of the drum (its internal management). The important thing is to keep in step. The very mechanism of the parade itself prevents most participants from getting an overview of how the parade is functioning. Most participants, as a result, remain at a pre-critical level. By criticism we mean not nit-picking, name-calling, or rock-throwing, but rather an evaluation that leads to emancipation. But at this level people act in a non-evaluative way.

We can sum up the traditional appropriation of faith by saying that it comes from the *outside-in*. It's as though when a person was baptized, someone put a spiritual knapsack on his or her back. This has gradually been filled up with in-doctrination and socialization as the person marched in the support parade. It is basically a passive acceptance of faith life. Although one may work very hard at marching, still the acceptance of one's place in the parade is primarily passive. It is an appropriation of faith from without.

Transitional (One model)

A radical change takes place as one moves to this second level of appropriation. The person experiences a deep spiritual and psychological need to reach back into the knapsack, to take out one's faith, to examine it closely, to go through an agonizing reappraisal, to personalize and authenticate that faith, and to place it in one's heart so that now one's faith begins to emanate from the *inside-out* rather than from the outside-in. "To place it in one's heart" is not mere pious rhetoric; rather, it expresses a radical change in the way one appropriates his or her faith, analogous to what the convert goes through on the way to conversion to the Christian faith. Appropriation changes from primarily passive, external, outside-in to primarily active, internal, inside-out possession of one's faith life values.

There are many models or ways by which this shift in appropriation can take place. Here are just a few:

Head ---------- Heart

Group ---------- Individual

Interior ---------- Exterior

Notice that the models come in pairs. For every model there is an "opposite" model — not in the sense of contradictory but in dialectical tension with each other. Let us examine each of these models.

Head Model: The person appropriates his or her faith in a very rational, logical manner. One "thinks" through one's faith as the internal appropriation takes place. Premises are examined, logic is scrutinized, internal consistency is demanded. Of course, in real life no one ever goes through this process in a totally rational, non-emotive fashion; people are more than minds, especially where religious commitments are involved. Nevertheless, in this model the intellectual dimension predominates.

Heart Model: This is basically an intuitional process. Intuitional is not to be confused with a purely emotional process. Emotions alone can be here today and gone tomorrow. One of the great things that the Orient can teach us is that intuition is the intelligence operating at a higher level, arriving at openness and love commitment without explicitly plodding through the usual conceptual process.

Group Model: This is the one we are most familiar with in recent times. People join a group (study group, prayer group, service team . . . the list is endless) and together they internalize the appropriation of faith life values. Often they are aided by an entrance process specific to that group.

Individual Model: Here the encounter is more of a one-to-one, heart-to-heart, eyeball-to-eyeball process with God (Christ) and the implications of his message.

Interior Model: The prime focus is on one's own interior spirituality and prayer life.

Exterior Model: Here the prime focus is on service to others: the poor, the sick, the elderly, the deprived.

Generally, when a person's faith begins to emanate from the inside-out, one model predominates. Although more than one model may be incorporated, there is great reluctance to use two "opposite" models at this time. It's just too much too soon.

It is understandable that the person becomes enthusiatic over his or her breakthrough into a new level of faith appreciation. Our friend is enthralled with the model that has been encountered and experienced. But this can lead to difficulties. A characteristic of this level of faith appreciation is the tendency to be one-sided, to be given to dichotomy: "Either you resonate with my model or you are an outsider." Elitism may rear its ugly head, or at least a kind of spiritual exclusiveness. The person may be something of a Johnny One Note.

The quantum leap of Christianity includes millions of Christians who either have already made the passage from traditional to transitional appropriation of faith or are in the process of so doing. This passage may begin as early as mid-adolescence, but is by no means limited to the young. People from sixteen to ninety-six are taking part.

This level of faith appropriation is called transitional because in the best of all possible worlds it *should* be transitional. But for many it has become a permanent condition. It can, however, be the gateway to a higher level.

Integrated (Many models)

At this level the person uses many models to appropriate his or her faith. But there is more involved than just a multiplicity of models. For every model used, a spiritual and psychological need is felt to use the "opposite" model as well. And so the individual now is a person who can deal with dialectic and paradox, who can go beyond "either-or" to "both-and." This is not to be confused with a wishy-washy person who collapses toward a lukewarm theological middle. What we have here is a highly integrated, liberated, mature Christian. The tension experienced is not a debilitating nervous tension but a liberating creative tension. By drawing on many models in dialectical tension with one another, the person now begins to uncover much of the adventure and romance possible in the Christian experience. We shall see in the next chapter that it is people operating at this level who will be the key to successful ministry from now on.

This level is, of course, open-ended. As creative tension unfolds and the person grows in integration, liberation, maturity and deep-seated peace, a mystical quality appears. One thinks of the heroic bishop from El Salvador, Oscar Romero. Confronted by unbelievable outrages against social justice and peace, this man of God and servant of his people, in spite of threats from enemies without and insults from functionaries within, underwent the process outlined here. It culminated in active mysticism, sublime prophecy and martyrdom at the altar in the midst of the Eucharist.

By no means are we dealing with the whole of faith growth, but rather with one component: the way one appropriates or takes possession of one's faith. For centuries, in order to have a vigorous spirituality and an effective ministry, it sufficed to attain the traditional level of appropriation. Alas, those days are gone forever. For increasing numbers of people, growth in faith demands a move from external to internal appropriation. It's a brand new ball game!

What caused this quantum leap? Of the many causes, let us consider a few.

World War I and II. It was really one war with a twenty-year truce in between. There was a complete shift in mindset, most noticeably in Europe, from pre-1914 to post-1945. The Victorians and the Edwardians felt they had a firm grasp on reality and saw the world as an orderly, rational cosmos whose secrets were being opened up to science. In their view, everything had been named, and only a few blank spaces remained to be filled in. This optimism was shattered, and the wreckage was discernible in a thousand ways, perhaps most strikingly in the realms of art and philosophy. Existentialism was born of the experience of aloneness, of being cast adrift — cut off from the comfortable certainties and unchallenged loyalties of the recent past.

The Nuremberg Trials. These told the world that you can no longer use as a blanket excuse, the explanation "I was following the orders of my legal superiors." It may be a correct procedure in most cases, but the spectacle of defendants using it to justify war crimes of unspeakable gravity and even genocide showed, once and for all, that unquestioning obedience and loyalty can sometimes be even more destructive than disobedience and revolt. After the holocaust, the good citizen had to be redefined. There is a higher law that puts limits on our loyalty to any authority that is not God.

Vatican II. This was basically a call to move from external to internal appropriation of faith. Pioneer theologians who had been under suspicion and even silenced for decades, were not only rehabilitated but vindicated; and their ideas became normative for the new directions taken by the church. This council, which was pastoral rather than dogmatic, looked beyond the church to the wider world, and identified itself with some of the most progressive movements of the age.

The Vietnam War. It is not our purpose here to discuss the rightness or wrongness of America's role in that conflict. But there was so much controversy over it that a large segment of the American population could no longer follow political and military authorities in an uncritical way. People of both left and right, hawks as well as doves, were forced to evaluate what their leaders were doing. Part of our loss of innocence was the loss of faith in the myth of our own goodness.

The Civil Rights Struggles. In the face of patently unjust discriminatory laws, civil disobedience became for many not only legitimate but morally imperative. When Rosa Parks, a black woman, was arrested for refusing to surrender her seat on a bus to a white man, events were set in motion that not only won recognition of black people's civil rights but also forced people to rethink their attitudes toward authority and law. Martin Luther King, writing from a Birmingham jail that unjust laws had to be broken, helped millions of his fellow Americans to discover their consciences and take them seriously.

Instant Communications. There is no idea or event that cannot circle the globe within the hour. Once consciousness is raised in our time, it spreads rapidly. Oppressive powers can arrest, slander, defame, condemn and kill, but they cannot prevent the spread of the influence of a group like Solidarity. The latter is strong not only because it has influence in Poland, but because it has influence *outside* Poland. The silence of the victims is deafening and reverberates throughout the world. Within the church, new ideas circulate, are popularized, and spark debates that are no longer the private preserve of church leaders and scholars; and those ideas cannot be suppressed without evoking immediate worldwide reaction.

Jesus Christ. Now we really get to the heart of the matter. The primary cause of the quantum leap is a new attentiveness of Christians around the world to the call of the risen Christ, as he summons them to move from external to internal appropriation of faith. People today are discerning the divine call from Jesus more than their ancestors discerned it, precisely because of the many factors listed above. At his bidding, they are reaching into their spiritual knapsacks, striving to personalize and authenticate their Christian commitment. Christ is raising the stakes, putting more poker chips on the card table of life. He is raising the spiritual temperature of the globe. In fact, this quantum leap is bigger than Christianity. God is challenging people of all faiths and value systems to reach into their personal knapsacks and begin this adventure.

Within Christianity itself, people are far from approaching this adventure in a consolidated way. Churches, nations, dioceses, parishes, schools, religious communities and individuals vary in their degree of movement or (sigh!) non-movement. Some approach it eagerly, some reluctantly; some pretend it is not there. Many, unfortunately, have yet to be challenged. But to ignore this quantum leap, or to be responsible for others ignoring it, is something we do at our own peril and the peril of those we serve in ministry.

Let us begin to examine the many implications of this quantum leap.

3
WHERE ARE WE GOING?

Implications for Future Church

If we are going to respond to the call of Christ and take the quantum leap with him and his people, we must join in the shift from external to internal appropriation of faith. We can seek security by staying where we are, but it will be a false security, because the world will have left us behind.

In every parish and community there are elderly spiritual giants who may not want to come with us on this journey. They deserve our respect and consideration, for we stand on their shoulders and are indebted to them for what we are today. If they wish to continue to seek union while remaining at a traditional appropriation level, that's fine. No one has the right to snatch the novena booklets from their hands. It should be mentioned, however, that one of the authors has been threatened by senior citizens who promise they will punch his lights out if he tries to cut them out of the action. One religious superior has said that the problem is not with the elderly but with those in their 40's, 50's and 60's. They were trained for both spirituality and ministry at the traditional level. They now resent being called upon to make a mid-course correction at a time when they are peaking in their abilities.

Whether we like it or not, with every tick of the clock it becomes more necessary to move to an internal appropriation of faith for a viable and vibrant Christian existence. The fundamental question for ministry now becomes: How do I help myself and the people I serve attain an internal appropriation of faith?

From now on, to do ministry well it will be necessary to strive to attain the integrated level of faith appropriation. It is not that a person cannot do ministry prior to attaining this level, but the person must at least aspire to it, convinced that he or she will serve so much more effectively. Why is this so? Because today there is a three-way tension within Christianity. It can be found in the church (as a whole), diocese, parish, school faculty and even extended family. Consider the following diagram:

transitional   transitional

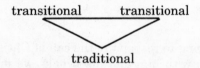

traditional

People at the transitional level and those at the traditional level often do not get along well together. They tend to talk "apples and oranges" to one another in a dialogue of the deaf. The transitional, filled with excitement about the new model of appropriation, tends to grab the traditional by the lapels and exclaim, "Everything new is good and everything old is bad." The traditional looks at this "radical" with a jaundiced eye and takes on a siege mentality: "Put the wagons in a circle; the Indians are attacking." This is a caricature, of course, but as in every caricature there is a bit of reality. The dynamics inherent in each of these two different modes of faith appropriation make dialogue and understanding extremely difficult.

Moreover, the tension doesn't end there. Transitionals clinging to opposite models don't get along well, either. For example, a transitional using an interior model views those using an exterior model and observes, "I grant you they do a lot of service but I think they are just humanitarians. They don't pray to the degree that we do." Our friend in the exterior model mutters something about those people sitting in a circle, holding hands, and never reaching out to serve. Again, we are looking at a caricature. But, as the caricature indicates, the dynamics peculiar to each model create tension for both parties. As with the case of the traditionals vs. the transitionals, this is the stuff of polarization. And we have seen more than enough of it in the past twenty years.

The three-way conflict pictured above indicates the need for the integrated level in ministry. The minister at the integrated level is often able to challenge the traditional without being threatening. Not always, of course, for no one can control either God's grace or human free will. But the integrated-level minister is often a better enabler in bringing God's grace and free will together.

Ministry operating at an integrated level also works better among transitionals. The one model already in use can be affirmed, but a whole new world of many models of faith appropriation can be opened up. Along with this comes the challenge of moving on to many models, some of which are in dialectical tension with the original model. Thus, for example, the activist can be encouraged to cultivate the interior life of prayer without sacrificing the thrust toward social concern and service. The person for whom conscience, individuality and responsibility have become important values can be challenged to make a new synthesis of these with values like obedience, loyalty and community.

Even in early adolescence (grades seven, eight and nine), problems can begin to occur. Although these youngsters are still quite dependent and operating at the traditional level, many have their ear to the ground and sense the movement that is taking place in Christianity. They cannot articulate this to anyone, even themselves, but they are already aware of it. If they now observe that their usual significant others — parents, teachers, sisters, brothers, priests — are at the traditional external level of faith appropriation, *these persons gradually*

24 So You Want To Do Ministry?

cease to be significant others for these youngsters, at least in
the matter of religion. There now appears a new significant
other, the peer — the kid in the crowd with the loudest voice,
the biggest mouth, the verbal bully. Down through the centuries
we have had parent and priest on one side, and peer on the
other side, striving for the loyalty of the adolescent. Priest and
parent used to win eight out of ten, but now they're lucky if
they win five out of ten. And things will get worse before they
get better, so long as parent, teacher or other religious guide
remains at the traditional appropriation level.

Adolescents always demand a lot from the important adults
in their lives, and their expectations are often unreasonable.
But perhaps even less than in earlier generations do they expect
these adults to be perfect or to have all the answers. What they
seem to be looking for, more than anything else, is authenticity.
This does not mean knowledge of the latest teenage songs,
dress trends or buzz words. It does mean honesty, admitting
one's limitations, respecting the young and not pulling rank on
them. It means resisting the temptation to overprotect their
children and their students, and being willing to take the risks
that go with respecting their freedom. But all this requires that
the older person knows where the mountain called Christianity
has moved and is willing to go with the flow.

This is the first generation of parents in centuries who cannot
pass on their faith to their children in the same way that it
was passed on to them. For as long as anyone can remember,
all a Christian parent had to do was ask, "How did my parents
bring me up in the faith?" and then decide, "I will do the same
for my children." And it worked. But not anymore.

From mid-adolescence on, people can begin to experience a
need to move from external to internal appropriation of faith.
This is not a phenomenon peculiar to youth; it applies to persons
from sixteen to ninety-six. If the church doesn't help them to
advance from traditional to transitional, they will often do it
on their own, choosing what we may call the "rejection" model.
They internalize their value system but in the process they

turn their spiritual knapsack upside down. Listen to Debbie, a young woman in her twenties:

> Years ago, people went to church because they were told to go by their parents and often led to church. But today people are free. A lot of us feel that we don't have to lean on religion. We think for ourselves. A person can be moral and truly religious without ever going to church. I am truly a freethinker.[1]

People like Debbie shake out what is in their knapsack and, in the process, leave the church. It would appear that millions have gone this route in recent years. They will not come back as long as the only manifestations of church they meet are at a traditional level of faith appropriation. To do so would be a kind of spiritual make-believe, even psychological suicide.

Two things have to happen before there can be a return. The person has to advance beyond the rejection model, not necessarily to the integrated level, but perhaps somewhere between. They must also encounter a manifestation of church (parish team or group, campus ministry) that is operating at the same level. Then there is hope of a rapprochement.

A problem similar to the one discussed above concerns many people in today's church who are at the transitional level and who make great contributions to ministry. They gradually experience a call to move on to the integrated level. If the church does not help them on the journey, there is a real possibility that they may drop out, at least from ministry and perhaps even from church attendance.

Another group of church members who need to move to transitional and integrated levels are many who belong to ethnic or racial minorities. They often experience a three-way tension that looks like this:

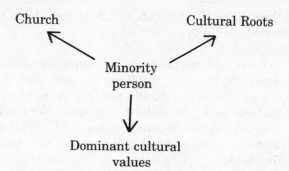

At the traditional level of faith appropriation, this person is being pulled in three different directions:

— *Church:* often operating at a traditional level, with a theology based on Greek philosophy and organized on a Roman concept of law; in short, a Graeco-Roman church hardly in tune with one's cultural roots.

— *Cultural Roots:* often lost or suppressed over the years, yet striving to come once more to the psychic surface.

— *Dominant cultural values:* embodied in ubiquitous, insistent media messages that are often hostile to and even destructive of the other two sets of values.

If the minority person is left by the church at the traditional level, the result may be a highly fragmented personality being called to march in three different parades which are apparently headed in three different directions. If able to operate only at a pre-evaluative level, the person may follow the significant others in one of the three parades and pay, at most, lipservice to the other two. Theoretically, two out of three can be lost to church membership.

Once faith is internalized, however, this fragmentation can begin to disappear. The person can rediscover the treasures in one's church and, at the same time, challenge the church to broaden its vision and change its structures. The person can begin to reappropriate his or her culture and, at the same time, subject it to constructive criticism. And the messages of the dominant culture can be seen for what they are — a mix of good and bad.

A close look at today's parish reveals that it contains many small groups — prayer, service, study . . . the variations are endless. Some have popular names, some have no name at all; but they all contribute to the vitality of the whole. The ideal parish of the future will be a community of communities, but it can easily become a collection of cliques. The direction it takes will depend largely on the quality of leadership of each group. If the leaders are at a traditional level, they may produce a ghetto. At a transitional level, they run the risk of promoting a one-model group that collapses in on itself. But leaders at the integrated level can avoid the pitfalls, bring out the best in the various groups, and invest the parish with a fuller overall dynamism.

There are many vigorous ministerial efforts in today's church — renewal, lay leadership, basic Christian community, evangelization outreach, vocations, justice and peace — to name just a few. To be successful, they must operate in an internalized faith appropriation milieu. Prior to the present quantum leap in Christianity, the sower could often safely assume that the soil was ready for ministerial seed. That has now become a fatal assumption. The messenger used to be able to take it for granted that the hearer could hear the message. Not any more. Unless messenger and hearer are operating at an internal appropriation level, they will get only twenty cents on the dollar. Burnout quickly follows.

To illustrate this, let us consider efforts for justice and peace. Each of us has a psychic searchlight that extends just so far. Within the range of that searchlight we are (or try to be) loving, caring people. But beyond the range, things get extremely murky. It's not that we resolve to be unloving, uncaring people as regards "out there." It's just that "out there" is literally *out there* — in effect, it doesn't exist. Third world atrocities are just sad stories on page four or five of the newspaper. Internal appropriation of faith increases the searchlight's range. The deeper the internalization, the broader the range and the more intense the beam.

Serious commitment to justice and peace must inevitably confront the need for systemic change. In some places in the world fifty per cent of the children never celebrate their fifth birthday. Why? Because they are dead. Why are they dead? Because of a variety of diseases. Why such a susceptibility to disease? Because of malnutrition. Why such malnutrition? Because the family breadwinner is not making a living wage. Although there is wealth within the economic system, it is being drained off either by a few private individuals or by the political system.

Love for these children demands not only medical help but also dealing with the sources of the problem. And that means a call for systemic change. And here is where the problem appears. When people at the traditional level of faith appropriation hear a call for systemic change, they tend to get upset and, consciously or unconsciously, resist the call. But justice is often unattainable without such change, whether it be political, economic, social or religious. Yet they resist, often stridently. Why? Because the notion of systemic change undermines the psychological structure of external faith appropriation, which asssumes that systems and parades don't change. Until ministry helps them attain internal appropriation, they simply will not hear.

We are an Exodus Generation called by the risen Christ to cooperate with him in the transformation of God's people. It is the call that was heard by the original Exodus heroes of the Old Testament, by the generation that encountered an itinerant missioner named Jesus of Nazareth, by the first generations of the infant church. Today people are hearing the call afresh, in a new way, and are responding to it in a way not unlike the people of the Exodus. It may help ministers to keep in mind that Moses probably had to drag a good number of the Israelites into the desert and that some of them would not leave.

In the last remaining years of the twentieth century our ministerial mission is to lay the foundation for the third millenium of Christianity. This calls not for cosmetic change but for quantum leap. Perhaps the crucial question Christ will ask each member of the church — from top to bottom — is not what was contributed to *maintenance ministry* but what was contributed to *transformational ministry*.

Let us begin to examine how we and the people we serve can make the journey from external to ever-deepening internal appropriation of our Christian faith.

---

[1]. "The Inquiring Fotographer" by Jimmy Jemail, the New York Daily News, Feb. 3, 1970.

Part Two: Prescription

4
HOW DO WE GET THERE?

A New Kind of Ministry

No patient was ever cured by diagnosis without taking the medicine prescribed. The diagnosis offered in Part One of this book does not solve our ministerial problems, but it does delineate more clearly what the problems are and helps us understand what is happening to us. What is needed now is a prescriptive game plan: a ministerial process which will enable us and the people we serve to move from external to internal appropriation of our faith and, with God's help, to grow in union with Christ and with one another.

Christian Discovery Process. The Holy Spirit often works in strange ways and uses what seem, to our eyes, the most unlikely instruments to give us ever deeper insights into Christian existence. In this instance the original insights into the process we are about to share with you came from non-Christians gradually working their way toward Christianity. Working in Japan, where less than one per cent of the population is Christian, we lived with these non-Christians, listened to them, told them about Christ and helped them come to faith in him.

Watching these dramas of grace and reflecting on these

stories of conversion, we came to see that in a twentieth century setting in the Far East the dynamics of first century, New Testament Christianity were operating once again. We knew at the outset that the art of ministry is to facilitate the coming together of God's grace and human free will, and that the minister can control neither one. The challenge was to create situations whereby the two could meet freely and deeply encounter each other. It gradually became apparent that what was happening was a series of search and encounter experiences which were in the deepest sense supernatural and yet followed a kind of natural order. The experiences were interlocking and cumulative, and can be described thus:

Christian
Discovery
Steps
                                    10. Omega: Kingdom

                              9. Entering into a deeper
                                    spirituality

                           8. Christian activity: filling
                                    out the implications

                        7. Baptism: a deeper meaning

                     6. Acceptance of God entering
                           the human condition

                  5. Realization that one cannot succeed
                        by self alone; God's reply
                           through Scripture

               4. Encountering God and others (practice)

            3. Encountering God and others (theory)

         2. Searching

      1. Preliminary

At the lowest level, the journey has not yet begun. Perhaps the person does not believe in God or is not even interested. The question either has not been raised or has been shelved as unimportant. Attitudes here may range from apathy to hostility, but the result is the same: a religious vacuum. Things begin to happen when, for some reason, a seeking person emerges. The search may be for God or for friendship or for love, or simply for some larger meaning; but it helps the person to break out of the prison of self-absorption.

The early stages of seeking mark a movement from a theoretical admission of a need for God to a practical commitment to action. The quest is frustrated and the process stalled until there occurs the breakthrough realization that success is impossible by human effort alone without God's help, and that this help has come with God's gracious initiative as expressed in Scripture and embodied in Jesus Christ.

Baptism now becomes not a merely traditional ceremony but the freely chosen acceptance of an offer of new life. The pilgrim becomes an active member of the church community and is invited and encouraged to enter into a deeper spirituality. With God's help, the journey will find its climax when the kingdom of God is realized in its fullness, in the transformation of the universe into heaven.

This brief description is not meant to imply a rigid, mechanistic approach to ministry. There is no way that either the Holy Spirit or the human spirit can be boxed in. Nevertheless, it is a valid description of the steps that many non-Christians and born Christians have taken to deeper union with God and others. Although this process was first observed and described in a Japanese setting, it has since been affirmed by people in a wide variety of ministerial settings both in the United States and in various places on five continents. A more detailed description of this process is the focus of the rest of this book.

Inductive Ministry. The concern of the Christian Discovery Process is the genesis of a deeper desire to encounter God and others. The goal is the resulting encounters themselves. Much of the ministry in practice today is still primarily deductive. It starts with lofty teachings and works downward. But what is the best way to unfold the implications of $E = mc^2$? Is it to start with $E = mc^2$ or to start with $2 + 2 = 4$? The Christian Discovery Process is inductive, with each step offering possibilities for presenting catechetical and theological content. The deductive approach, on the other hand, is often greeted with a yawn. The inductive process carries within itself its own motivation for acquiring catechetical and theological content — the desire to understand more fully the encounters already experienced and the desire to meet God and others on an even deeper level.

An excellent example of the inductive process is afforded by the story of Emmaus in Luke's 24th chapter. It appears to have its roots not only in a post-resurrection episode but also in the life stories of many who entered and lived in the early Lucan church. It may well be not only a dramatic account of a day in the lives of two disciples but a paradigm story of the experiences of many Christians. Christ first elicits from the disciples their hopes (Jesus is Messiah), their sorrows (Jesus has been killed), their fears (for their own lives, they are getting out of town — fast), and their chauvinism (the women's report of a risen Jesus is to be rejected). In short, he enables them to hear their own life stories. Only then does he unfold for them the Jesus story, that the Messiah passes through suffering unto glory.

I cannot hear the Jesus story in depth until I have heard my own story in depth. Only then can my story become part of the Jesus story and his story become part of mine. In the Emmaus account we see this symbolized with sacramental overtones in the breaking of the bread. The story culminates in ministry with the bringing of the good news of the risen Christ to others. What we have here is a classical example of inductive ministry. The Christian Discovery Process closely parallels it.

Christian Discovery: Core Ministerial Process. Christian Discovery is a *core* process because with fine tuning it can be applied to a wide variety of ministries. Since it is applicable for people from 16 to 96, it can be used in the upper high school years. But we have also found that teachers in grades one to ten are interested in the material. It gives them an idea of the seeds they are to plant in the minds and hearts of younger children so that they can come to fruition later on. It gives them a goal to aim at in their ministry to the young.

The process is also helpful in doing faculty renewal. In these changing times, schools sometimes lose their sense of mission. They can become mere collections of classes. And yet we realize that a school is greater than the sum of its parts. The process helps teachers do renewal not only as individual Christians but also as members of a team. The staff can thus regain a sense of unity, a sense of mission.

The Christian Discovery Process can contribute to a theology program at the college level. But its application extends beyond the classroom, and can be an effective instrument in campus ministry.

When we come to the parish, the applications are manifold. When we observe the average parish team today, we are looking at haggard people juggling 15 ministerial plates in the air at one time. And every time they open the mail from the chancery office or attend another meeting, they do so with fear and trembling because it could mean one more item to juggle in their ministerial week. What the parish team needs is a sense of synthesis: using one process for many ministerial endeavors. The process proposed will help them to do religious education (youth and adult), parish renewal, evangelization outreach, family ministry, lay leadership training, justice and peace awareness . . . the list is almost endless.

Today's parish contains a wide variety of groups — prayer groups, study groups, service groups. Some of these have an initiation process that is well thought out and functioning effectively. In cases like this, the Christian Discovery Process should be used not now but later, as a follow-up to the initiation process. It will reinforce the initiation experience and give it a new dimension, and can be especially helpful in the ongoing formation of the group's leaders.

In many places the new Rite of Christian Initiation of Adults

(RCIA) is used extensively both as a process for bringing new people into the church and as a vehicle for parish renewal. Excellent material is available which carefully explains the RCIA process and the principles on which it operates. (On examination we see that the RCIA calls for an inductive approach not unlike Emmaus.) The material also gives an excellent treatment of the liturgical highlights that take place as the process unfolds. Unfortunately, there is not much material concerning what to do, week in and week out, as we take people through the RCIA process. The Christian Discovery Process responds to this need (cf. Appendix for further elaboration).

Finally, the Christian Discovery Process can be very useful in contributing to the formation of people preparing to do ministry. The very process that was part of their formation can then, in turn, be used by these new people when they actually enter ministry. And so the Christian Discovery steps can be both a formational and a ministerial process. Let us now begin to examine this process in detail.

5
IS THAT ALL THERE IS?

The Primal Cry for More

Preliminary (Step One)

The preliminary situation from which the Christian Discovery process starts varies from individual to individual. Is the person starting at the traditional level of faith and beginning the journey from external to internal appropriation? Or is it a journey from the transitional (one model) level toward an integrated (many models) faith appropriation? Or might it be from the integrated level towards the open-ended high reaches of faith appropriation with its characteristics of mysticism and a signficant prophetic element? Besides the above, an almost infinite variety of personal characteristics and life situations can contribute to the various concrete descriptions. Yet along this wide spectrum of experience, let us simply say that the preliminary step is where the person finds herself or himself at the moment with a potential for beginning.

The most difficult move in the Christian Discovery Process is the one from preliminary (Step One) to searching (Step Two). Newton's laws of motion seem to apply to the spiritual life as well as to classical physics. "A thing not in motion tends to remain at rest; a thing once in motion tends to remain in motion." It is often very hard for the person at the traditional faith appropriation level to leave the security of a unity-by-uniformity parade and begin the journey toward internal faith possession. Likewise, the person at the transitional (one model) level may find it most difficult to move on to many models, some of which are in dialectical tension with the original model which the person values as a spiritual treasure. Such a move may appear threatening because it seems to undermine the original breakthrough. In the same way, it must also be arduous for the person at the integrated faith level to begin again and venture into the still mostly unchartered upper reaches of faith appropriation.

What is it that helps people get off the dime and begin to become searching persons? Spiritual inertia (Why bother?) is a powerful motive for hunkering down in the status quo. Argumentation doesn't work. Exhortation alone doesn't seem to accomplish much, either. The diagnosis and its implications given in the first part of this book helps, but for most people it's going to take more than that. It's going to take the primal cry for more, the primal cry for meaning.

The Primal Cry for More (Step Two)

The best motivation for moving from preliminary (Step One) to searching (Step Two) comes from inside the person. It is one's own heart crying out for fulfillment. We ask the person to look deep into his or her heart: What are the deepest longings, the fondest hopes, the most cherished desires of your heart? The person is called upon to surface and expand his or her basic heart wishes. Thus is elicited the primal cry for more.

This is not easy to do. Many people, surprisingly, seem to be afraid of joy and happiness. Why is this? Perhaps there is a certain security in being miserable. At least you know exactly where you are. "I was miserable yesterday, I'm miserable today, I plan to be miserable tomorrow." On the other hand, if joy enters your life, your moods may go up and down the scale. Some people prefer security to happiness. Others have an almost pathological fear of joy. Many young people today engage in disturbingly anti-social and self-destructive activities. If you could get inside their collective psyche and look out, you would be peering down a tunnel. For all their exaggerated actions, they are often trapped inside very narrow heart wishes. Their problem is not wanting too much but too little.

It takes courage then to surface and to *expand* one's basic heart wishes. And so we turn to the Personal Evolution Process:

1. Do a review of your life;

2. Surface and expand your basic heart wishes;

3. Try to attain these.

A review of one's life is not to be confused with an examination of conscience. It is, rather, a non-threatening review of one's existence. Was I born short or tall, rich or poor, with or without a good singing voice? What has unfolded in the twenty, thirty, forty, fifty years of my life? The purpose of this review is to provide the background for the second part.

There appear to be four basic heart wishes. The list, of course, is not carved in stone; one could make a case for a longer or shorter list. But after submitting it to many people in a variety of places and cultures, we have found that pastorally it works. What they say, in effect, is, "Yes, around these four themes I seem to be able to assemble the deepest longings of my heart."

The four basic heart wishes are:

1) to love,

2) to be loved,

3) to share,

4) to blossom out.

These are not four separate boxes. Rather, think of a diamond slowly turning so that one facet gradually blends into the next. Consider the first two: to love and be loved. It is probably impossible to define love; it is too intimate, too much a part of us. We can see everyone else's face in a room except our own; it is too close. So we cannot pick love up, put it under a microscope and examine it. Instead of defining it, let us attempt a working description. *To love* and *be loved* involves a forgetting of self, a leaping out of self toward the other to increase the other's joy (and, paradoxically, often increase my own). Nor does it focus only on joy. If the beloved is experiencing a sorrow, a hurt, a loneliness, I try to remove it. If that is not possible, I attempt to diminish it. If even that is impossible, I say to the other: "Give me half. You are not alone. We're in this together."

This reaching out to the other concerns not only the highs and lows of joy and sorrow, but even the ordinary, prosaic experiences of life. Humdrum things like waiting for a bus or cleaning a floor suddenly take on a feeling of adventure when done with someone we love. More wonderful still, the beloved is reaching out to me to increase my joy, lessen my sorrow, share simple, humble things with me and make them come alive. Isn't this the relationship we want with Christ? With one another?

To share means to take part in the experiences and deepest feelings of others and to have them, in turn, enter into my experiences and emotions. A more communitarian term for sharing is "solidarity," with all the overtones that word now carries.

To say that we want *to blossom out* means that there are many seeds within us that we would like to see come to full flower, many potentialities that we would like to see come to fulfillment. In more communitarian terms, it could well refer to a community hemmed in by political, economic, social or (sad to say) religious injustice that strives to attain its full potentialities.

Expanded heart wishes can never be attained by self alone. With narrow heart wishes, it is possible to collapse back into self and remain in stultifying isolation, reaching out occasionally to use others for my own selfish ends. Even God can be used this way, in certain kinds of religious formalism. Because we are by our very nature programmed for infinity, we can attain expanded heart wishes only by reaching out to an Other and to others — to God and the people in our lives.

The Primal Cry for Meaning (Step Two continued)

People come in different personal packages, so the way they initiate the search process varies from person to person. There is another basic heart wish in all of us, often deeply hidden. It is the existential need to address questions of ultimate concern. It may be buried deep within us, hidden by a kind of religiosity that prevents us from addressing the most serious questions that we can put to life.

Religiousness is an extremely complex phenomenon which does not lend itself to facile, simplistic analysis. People practice religion and join churches and synagogues and temples and cults and sects for a variety of reasons. They may do so out of habit, or superstition, or fear, or guilt. They may simply be seeking experiences of community, of solidarity, of a sense of belonging. They may be looking to channel their idealism, to find a scope for the expression of humanistic concern. Or they may want something not for themselves but for their children — an island of stability, a source of values, a teacher of morality and discipline. And often, in the same person, some or all of the above motives may be mingled in conscious and unconscious ways.

In this incomplete list of religious and quasi-religious motivations there is obviously a good deal of chaff mingled with the wheat. Religion is not always a healthy phenomenon. It can ennoble people and their institutions and cultures, but it can also be a force for narrowness, complacency or bigotry. Even where the religious phenomenon is clearly life-enhancing and brings out people's better qualities, it is clear that at different times and in different place some motivations are more effective than others. For example, in a closed or traditional society, habit and response to social pressure keep members on church rolls and deliver the approved behaviors. In a more open or

pluralistic milieu, other influences may be needed to insure
loyalty and encourage commitment.

At any rate, the basic heart wishes underlie the sturdier
manifestations of religiousness. But how are these heart wishes
expressed? Often they surface when people seek a larger sense
of significance in their lives. They go beyond the pragmatic and
the profane and put more fundamental questions to existence.
These are questions of ultimate meaning. Are we alone in the
universe, or is there Someone in charge? Is there any transcendent purpose to human life? Is existence ultimately comedy or
tragedy? What is the strongest force in the universe — life, or
death? How does a good man or woman behave?

Andrew Greeley says that these are the questions that Jesus
came to answer.[1] His answers are clear and forthright. We are
not alone; we have a Father in heaven who watches over us.
Our lives are not without purpose; we are meant to share in
God's own life. No failure need be final, no disaster irretrievable,
provided we accept God's offer of grace. Life will surely triumph,
as Jesus has won the definitive victory over sin and death. And
we are called to share in this victory by loving one another.

These are the answers that Jesus gives to the most profound
questions we can put to life. As evangelists and ministers, we
are eager to preach this good news. But it is useless to offer
people answers to questions that they have not asked. But
doesn't everyone ask these questions? Maybe. There seem to
be people around who seldom or never ask them, whose attention and energies are totally taken up with the more immediate,
pressing concerns that occupy us all — to make a living, pursue
a career, raise a family, pay the bills. There is much in contem-
porary culture which inhibits attention to the transcendent and
encourages absorption in the contingent present. But until one
asks such questions with existential concern, what meaning
can religion have? The great religions of the world are, at their
core, attempts to address the mystery at the center of life. They
have gained adherents and enriched people's lives because they
offered them a way to deal with these cosmic concerns. Indeed,
the shallowness of much that passes for religion today may be

due in part to the fact that many people in church are not there to address these concerns. How many people join or stay in a church because they find there the solution to the most profound questions arising from the human condition?

This issue is dealt with in a striking way in a brief film, *The Red Kite*.[2] Fred, a young husband and father, has a disturbing encounter with a drunken, middle-aged priest on a bus ride home from work. As they pass a cemetery, the tipsy cleric shocks his fellow passengers by musing aloud: "It's all a sham. They're in there for good. And that's the end of it." Troubled, Fred seeks to confide in his wife in their bedroom that night. He reveals his sense of failure and personal insignificance, fears dredged up by the priest's despair. "I am the most ordinary of men, leading the most ordinary of lives." But she is unable to respond, whether out of her own repressed fear or because she simply cannot relate to his anxiety. All she can say is: "You're not a failure. Don't talk like that! What's wrong with being ordinary . . just average people? We're doing quite well; we're doing as well as most. Anyway, I'm satisfied." And there the conversation ends — in total failure to communicate.

What makes this scene even more interesting is the fact that, earlier in the evening, she indicates in a casual remark that she is a church-goer. Yet she is utterly unable to deal with a most basic religious question: Is death the end, or does life endure? This inability or refusal is the price she pays for her complacency. And we are left wondering about the role of religion in her life. Does it challenge or console in any significant sense? Does it ground her values, or lend depth or strength to her commitments? Or is it a purely conventional adornment, lending a surface respectability but leaving the deeper part of her untouched?

Fred, on the other hand, comes across as a deeply religious person in the root sense. Though we are given no hint of whether he belongs to or attends a church, he is a restless seeker of the transcendent. Indeed, he realizes that nothing less than a revelation from God will satisfy his hunger for meaning and life. From a Christian point of view, we can say that he is asking the questions Jesus comes to answer, and is longing for what Jesus comes to give. "I have come that they may have life, and have it more abundantly." (John 10:10). Later in the film, he does receive a revelation in the form of a sign. On a mountain top he sees, in his little daughter, what God has been trying to tell him all along.

Of course, asking questions of ultimate meaning does not guarantee that one will accept the answer given by God in Jesus Christ. Faith is free, and assent can be witheld. James Fowler relates an encounter he had sharing a taxicab from a New York City airport. His companion, an aspiring playwright, chided him: "You people — you clergymen and theologians — you're the ones who are responsible for most of our trouble. You try to convince people that they are more than animals. You try to make them believe that there is some kind of transcendent purpose to life, some kind of cosmic meaning that they can be part of." Later, he summed up his world view: "The way I see it, if we have any purpose on this earth, it is just to keep things going. We can stir the pot while we are here and try to keep things interesting. Beyond that everything runs down: your marriage runs down, your body runs down: your faith runs down. We can only try to make it interesting."[3]

We can disagree with this man, but at least he deserves our respect. He has not been afraid to ask the big questions, even if he has come up empty. In somewhat the same vein, though less reflectively, a young woman in Times Square responded to a journalist asking why fewer people go to church: "Is this really a fact? I'm surprised. I didn't think people were that intelligent. I see that you are surprised at my answer. Please don't be. Sir, I don't believe in religion. I believe in myself, my own inner thoughts of morality. I also believe that at the end of this life nothing remains but ashes."[4]

Here we see the danger of facing ultimate questions squarely. Perhaps it is this abyss that Fred's wife is shrinking from in *The Red Kite*. Is it possible that churchgoing itself can be part of a defense mechanism? Martin Marty once observed that some people use religion as a defense against the radical demands of faith. Jesus calls for more than a vague sense of well-being and a promise to be nice to one another. He makes the most dogmatic assertions and astounding promises, and offers no proof but himself. He invites us to go to the heart of the matter, to the core of existence. This is not a journey for the shallow of mind or the faint of heart. Fred's wife insulates herself against disappointment by not asking too much from life. "What's wrong with being ordinary? We're doing as well as most." Fred wants more. He asks for a sign that the priest is wrong, that Fowler's cab companion is mistaken. The beginning of ministry is not to answer questions of ultimate concern until we have helped people to ask them . . . to open themselves to the possibility not only of faith but also of despair. That is the risk we run, the high stakes for which we play.

Questions of ultimate concern, once asked, can never be answered in splendid isolation. There is a need to reach out to fellow seekers. We must reach out to an Other even if at this time the letter is sent to "Addressee Unknown." Having striven in the last part of this chapter to break through the crust of religiosity to the questions of ultimate concern, let us now ask ourselves, "What is religion?"

[1]*The Jesus Myth*, Andrew Greeley, Doubleday, 1971, pp. 48-49.

[2]National Film Board of Canada, 1965. Wombat Films, distributor.

[3]*Life Maps,* James Fowler and Sam Keen, edited by Jerome Berryman, Word Books, Waco, TX, 1978, pp. 22-23.

[4]Jimmy Jemail, "The Inquiring Fotographer," *New York Daily News,* Feb. 3, 1970.

6
RELIGION, ANYONE?

Reach Out and Touch Someone (Step 3)

What is religion? People are always talking about it, but what is it?

We are looking not for a theological definition but a working description. Most people have a working description at a conscious or subconscious level. Stop 100 people on Main Street and ask them what religion is, analyze their answers, and you will find that nearly all of them are saying pretty much the same thing with minor variations. It comes down to: "Religion is adhering to the sacred customs of my group." A sacred custom may be a credal formula, a moral code, a form of worship, a certain lifestyle, etc. Such a working description is a fairly accurate portrayal of what church membership means for most people. In times past it seems to have provided sufficient motivation to keep them saying their prayers, going to church, and contributing to religious institutions and causes. Unfortunately, for many people it doesn't work anymore.

To say this is not to deny the truth of the creed or the code or to denigrate the sacred customs of prayer and worship. It is simply recognizing a fact that can no longer be denied or ignored: that the working description of religion that many people carry within them no longer motivates them to practice their faith. Why is this?

The answer, of course, lies in the quantum leap from external to internal appropriations of faith. For centuries during which Christianity operated at the traditional level of faith appropriation, the parade phenomenon of unity-by-uniformity was predominant. Church members followed significant others in a non-evaluative way. It was difficult not to conform when they felt strong psychological pressure to march as others were marching. But for many people today, this pressure has almost disappeared. As a result, many go through an explicit or implicit line of reasoning something like this: "I don't feel a need to march in the footsteps of my religious forebears. I don't feel a need to adhere to those customs. Therefore I don't need religion." Well may you protest that the conclusion is incorrect. The fact remains that for millions it *is* the conclusion. Many will not cease religious practice altogether, but it is now reduced to serving as a social lubricant in the form of baptisms, weddings and funerals. Religion thus becomes a collection of tribal ceremonies surviving on the fringes of existence and exerting no significant influence on the values and commitments of people's day-to-day lives.

The effect of all this on the self-image of those in ministry is devastating. You're excited about something no one wants. You're providing a service for which people feel no need. You're a fire-fighter in a fireproof town.

A New Working Description

What we have to do, then, is go back to the drawing board and get a new working description of religion. In the radically altered situation in which we find ourselves, one that does justice to the reality and offers effective motivation is this: *The encountering of God and others, by which we attain our basic heart wishes.* In this definition, notice that the religious need is now emanating from the inside out. Religion can no longer be considered a "trip" laid on me by priest and parent. It now becomes the quest for the fulfillment of the primal cries of my heart, which can be realized only by reaching out beyond myself in encounter with God and others. To be religious, in this deeper sense, is to extend myself beyond myself — to God and others — in response to the primal cry for more (to love, to be loved, to share, to blossom out) and the primal cry for meaning (to address the questions of ultimate concern).

Nothing much is accomplished by putting this new working description of religion in next week's parish bulletin. More than mere information is required here. What is needed is a deeply personal experience of the primal cry for more. And this cry must arise from within the person, expressing a felt need for religious encounter, however clearly or dimly the object of that encounter is perceived. This is simply another way of saying that without Step Two, the cry for more, there can be no Step Three, the impulse to encounter God and others.

Religion: Dichotomy or Dialectic?

What prevents people from taking this step, from feeling and expressing this need to transcend themselves and to go out to others and the Other? The obstacles are many. For starters, there is secularization, which reduces life to a series of problems and projects and discourages even the articulation of questions of larger meaning. There is consumerism, which restricts human striving to the acquisition of material possessions and, in a triumph of trivialization, relegates any higher aspirations to the realm of the irrelevant. But sometimes the difficulty lies within religion itself, or rather in the way it is presented.

The presentation of religion in the past often unwittingly had a dichotomizing effect on the recipient. The question was asked, "Who wants to be Christ-centered?" And, of course, everyone's hand went up. Then came the question, "Who wants to be self-centered?" If your hand went up, you were in big trouble! Of course, the purpose was to get rid of self-centered-ness and selfishness; but many times, unfortunately, self also went out the window. Religion thus came to be perceived as Christ versus the Self, with unfortunate psychological results and a stultifying effect on the religious impulse.

This is no straw man that we are setting up here. The fear that in finding God we may lose ourselves runs deep in many of the people of our times. Jean-Paul Sartre, whose influence on twentieth-century people goes far beyond those who have heard of him and his atheistic existentialism, used to say that if God existed He would be everything and we would be nothing. For him, the death of God was a precondition for our coming alive. Recall the two young women quoted above: "Sir, I don't believe in religion; I believe in myself." "A lot of us feel we don't have to lean on religion; we think for ourselves." Such sentiments reveal a pervasive suspicion that religion involves not only self-denial but also the denial of self-worth. And to lend respectability to this suspicion there are always more than a few church people who are bad advertisements for a good cause. They build into their religious styles and expressions all kinds of unhealthy guilt, repression, and self-abasement. They lack even a healthy confidence in themselves and their basic instincts, and try to extol God by demeaning His creatures. How else explain the fact that in our day the word "humanism," which stands for respect for human dignity and concern for human welfare, has become a bad word in many religious circles?

The new working description of religion that we are proposing discourages this kind of false dichotomy and encourages a shift from an either/or to a both/and practice of religion. The greater the basic heart wishes, the greater the need to encounter God and others. The greater the encounters, the greater heart wishes and corresponding growth of the person. Encounter begets personal growth, personal growth begets encounter.

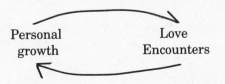

Personal growth   Love Encounters

Of course, the life-long struggle against selfishness goes on. And yet each call to love encounter is a challenge to rise above that selfishness. So if you want to be more religious (to encounter God and others), expand your basic heart wishes!

Do Not Pass Go

People in ministry, in their eagerness to share the good news of Scripture, Christ and church, often neglect to share first the good news of religion itself. What we are urging here is a return to basics in the truest sense. Until people have overcome any fear or suspicion they may have of religion in general, they will resist any specific religious message, no matter how attractive or appealing. Until they expand their heart wishes to ask for more, Scripture is unintelligible, Christ is superfluous, and church is at best a bore and a menace at worst.

Before the quantum leap, this oversight had minimal consequences, especially among born Christians. Religious instruction and exhortation on a Scripture-Christ-church level kept most people marching in the parade. After the quantum leap, such an oversight has disastrous consequences. Unless a solid foundation is laid for ministry at the level of religion, ministerial efforts at the level of Scripture, Christ and church will either come tumbling down with the crash of outright rejection or slowly sink into the quagmire of apathy with the yawn of boredom.

Let us now begin to examine how encounters with God and others take place.

7
HELP!

Where's Grace? (Step 4)

Encounter

What are the dynamics of encounter? To put it simply, you must *go out* in order to *meet*. Encounter involves a leap out of self toward the other. And it is scary. It involves an adventure. That is why we are all surrounded by innumerable acquaintances while deep friendships remain at a premium. It is easy to make an acquaintance but difficult to make a friend.

Consider the following diagram:

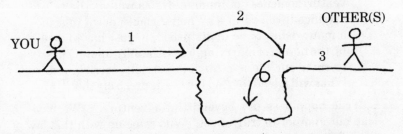

The first movement is not too difficult. It involves going from stranger to acquaintance. It's fairly easy to strike up acquaintanceships with others: work together, live in the same neighborhood, join the same clubs, etc. It's not too hard to become an acquaintance of God: all you have to do is observe a certain number of religious formalities. But now comes the scary part. Before you there looms a chasm over which you must leap in order to have an intimate friendship. The leap toward God is not an easy one. To strip off the protective covering of formality, to meet God in a face-to-face, lover-beloved relationship (with occasional lovers' quarrels) requires courage. Yet it appears to be a basic law of life that true happiness lies beyond the adventure. Intimacy is not attainable on the cheap. Likewise, the leap toward others is no mean task. It involves a willingness to reveal self and an openness to vulnerability. Oh, what vulnerability! For there is always the possibility of rejection. One is at the mercy of the other, and a push can send one tumbling into the chasm. Yet the true happiness we all seek is attainable only if we are willing to undergo the risk of adventure.

> When it comes right down to it, what puts you off is that once you set the wheels you don't know how far you're liable to go. No, this, we know very well, is what keeps those who do have faith from having more faith. We know, as Riviere put it so well, that "love involves staggering complications." We are always taking something upon ourselves when we introduce somebody else into our life, even from the human point of view. We know that no longer shall we be altogether our own man. Therein lies the adventuresomeness of human love as well as the self-sacrifice involved in it. When it comes down to it, if a man wishes to be undisturbed, he just has to give up the notion of marrying. Well, then! To allow Christ to enter our life is a terrible, terrible, terrible risk. What will it lead to? And faith — is precisely that.[1]

"True happiness lies beyond the adventure." "We have to leap out in order to truly meet." Who came up with this law of life? The answer, of course, is God. What should be our reaction? Well, some years ago one of the authors found himself visiting a mission in the jungles of Venezuela. A siesta in hammocks slung from trees left everyone hot and sticky. Nearby flowed a river which was looking cooler every minute, so he asked the local missioner about the possibility of a swim. The missioner was agreeable, but mumbled something about stingrays with poisonous tails, electric eels, and piranha fish. Our hero paused, then looked the missioner in the eye and said, "Okay. You first!"

And so we look God in the eye and say, "Okay. You came up with this law of life that adventure must come before true happiness. You first!" Well, God has gone first.

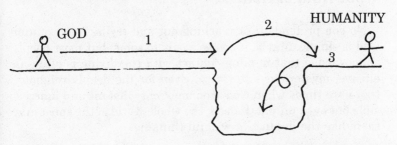

Isn't the Old Testament the story of moving from unknown God to well-known God? What better description of the Incarnation than the ultimate leaping out, the supreme encounter? God leaps out of the heavenly condition into the human condition.

> He always had the nature of God,
>> but he did not think that by force
>> he should try to become equal with God.
> Instead of this, of his own free will
>> he gave up all that he had,
>> and took the nature of a servant.
> He became like man
>> and appeared in human likeness.
> He was humble and walked the path of obedience
>> all the way to death —
>> his death on the cross.

> — *Phil. 2:6-8*

In doing so, the incarnate God experienced encounter with Mary, first and foremost, and then with many disciples-become-friends. (A footnote: if a new and vibrant Mariology is to be developed, perhaps it should start from two themes — Mary, mother of God, and Mary the encounter-er. What a gutsy young woman!) Besides the encounters, Jesus experienced the chasm to the fullest: rejection, defamation, abandonment, execution. All of this doesn't make encounter any less frightening but it is consoling to know that the Role Model found it scary, too.

What Kind of God?

No one pretends that reaching out and trying to encounter God is simple. Maybe it comes easily to some, but most people acknowledge that making contact with the divine is often an elusive, mysterious enterprise. Even for the deeply religious, there are times when God seems not only distant and inaccessible but even unreal. Indeed, the whole world of the spirit may seem like the product of wishful thinking.

As formidable as this difficulty is, however, it is not the only obstacle to opening ourselves to God's embrace, and it is probably not the most serious. There are other considerations, not often discussed in books like this one, which we ignore at our peril. They come down to this: God, for many potentially religious people, is not just mysterious or elusive or problematic. He is downright *threatening*. Besides being a riddle or puzzle that is hard for the mind to encompass or accept, he assaults the emotions with feelings of disquiet and even fear. This is not exactly the same phenomenon as Rudolph Otto's *mysterium tremendum et fascinans*. It is something much more negative, often beneath the level of consciousness, which can stifle the religious impulse in its cradle. It is the oft-unspoken fear that if we find God we will lose the best part of ourselves. Unlike thoroughly secularized persons who see religion as superfluous, these see it as a potential impoverishment of the self. To them, religion is not just a mistaken world view but a negative force that can make us less human.

To some unsophisticated, pious folks, this sounds like non-sense. How, they ask, can you think of God this way, when Jesus tells us that he is a loving Father who watches over us and cares for us? But there are many serious, open-minded people who know very well what we mean. And they are not all intellectuals and academicians. But they have experienced modernity and have absorbed a certain way of looking at and being in the world that evokes a palpable hostility to the transcendent.

Why is this so? We believe that this reaction cannot be understood or appreciated unless we listen seriously to the two great modern critics of religion: Sigmund Freud and Karl Marx. Their atheism is peculiarly *modern*. They are men who have helped to shape the world of the last two centuries because they were in touch with the minds and hearts of men and women in their times and ours. There are millions of people who know little more about these men than their names but who are deeply influenced by them. As a result, for reasons they cannot always articulate, they resist what Christians call Good News for the simple reason that it sounds like Bad News.

For Freud, God is someone invented to fulfill certain human needs. Small children in loving, healthy families possess a sense of security which adults might well envy. To the very young child, the parent is omnipotent — able to solve any problem, repel any danger, meet any crisis. This idealization of the parent suffers a mortal blow when children discover death and gradually realize that no one — not even their parents — can save them. How do they react to this first great loss of innocence? Freud says they have two choices: either accept life (and death) as they are and come to terms with the limitations of existence, or invent a surrogate Parent to replace the lost omnipotent parents. This Parent is called God, and is the product of wishful thinking. Thus, religion is seen as an infantile regression, a failure to grow. (Some teenagers reflect this thinking when they refer to religion as a "security blanket.")

Does Freud, then, condemn religion? Not totally. If it helps people cope with life better than they would otherwise, it is to be tolerated. But it would be better if they could deal with life as it really is, rather than the way they would like it to be. Accepting existence on its own terms is more adult and ultimately more honest. Moreover, religious people are notoriously vulnerable to manipulation, overdependence, rigidity and false guilt. It is undeniable that much of "man's inhumanity to man" has been inflicted in the name of God. And when we do not punish one another, we punish ourselves.

Is this an accurate, balanced portrayal of the whole religious scene? Of course not. Nor does it reflect the way all or maybe even most religious people think or feel about God. There is a whole world of religious experience and sentiment closed to Freud. Nevertheless, in the minds of many, his critique of religion is truly devastating. And so God is seen as a threat to human growth, as someone who, if we let him into our lives, will never let us grow up and live our lives to the full. Remember the young woman quoted earlier: "A lot of us feel that we don't have to lean on religion. We think for ourselves." In that same interview, another young woman said: "Sir, I don't believe in religion. I believe in myself."

It is not very difficult to marshal evidence in support of this view. There have always been and always will be people who find in religion an escape from life's harsh realities. This would be harmless except that they often find, in religion, all kinds of excuses for not doing things that need to be done. And this happens not only on the individual level but on the social level as well. Think of all the evil, man-made structures that have either been defended or allowed to endure in the name of religion. It is a sad but undeniable fact that most great social reforms occur either without much help from churchgoing folk or in spite of their inertia or opposition.

It is here that Marx complements the thought of Freud. The latter criticizes religion on psychological grounds, as stifling individual growth; the former rejects it on political grounds, for standing in the way of social reform. It is a tragic fact that in our own day many feel, consciously or unconsciously, that they have to make a choice between Christianity and humanism.

The Minister's Role

Just as in social justice it is necessary to do systemic analysis in order to understand what is really happening, so those in ministry must do a spiritual analysis of the environment in which they work. Are there misconceptions, perhaps at a subconscious level, about God? Is God perceived as one who views life in compartments and is concerned only with the spiritual, sacred, eternal dimensions of our lives, while material, secular, temporal concerns are ignored? When people think of God this way, should we introduce them to a God who takes a more holistic approach to life?

Distorted images of God produce perverted forms of religion and all kinds of false dichotomies. How many people think that God wants us to be holy in such a way that we must become less interesting personalities, so that holiness becomes synonomous with creepiness? Are they aware that if they do not love themselves they cannot love and give themselves to others? On the other hand, has legitimate love of self degenerated into selfishness? Does religious concern extend only to one's immediate group or does it reach out to the poor, the elderly, the sick, the lonely, the marginated? Does it extend to the Third World? Are our people aware of the power of political and economic policies, established by governments and multinational companies, to undermine life (and even take lives) in distant places?

All of this — to reach out to God and others, to develop a spirituality that values and affirms our humanity and that opens us up to life rather than shutting us off from it — has to be attempted both by the people we serve and by ourselves along with them. And yet. . . .

The Primal Cry for Help

And yet, although we talk a great game of religion over martinis at six in the evening, when we wake up at two in the morning, God has no face. He is not as real as the people we meet all day. We thought it would be easy to love people; just turn the rheostat of the heart from low to high. But it soon becomes apparent that it is very hard to love people. Also, it comes as a great shock that I'm not as lovable as I thought I was. So the attempt to put into practice the encountering of God and others (Step 4) culminates in the primal cry for help.

Notice the integration of the Christian Discovery Process so far:

— It culminates in the primal cry for help (Step 4),

— to have love encounters with God and others, which is what religion is (Step 3),

— in order to attain the basic heart wishes: to love, to be loved, to share, to blossom out, to address questions of ultimate concern (Step 2).

One of the great deficiencies in ministry today is to neglect — or to do in cursory fashion — these foundational steps. In these changing times, to do scripture-Christ-church ministry without this foundation is:

a) to answer questions that haven't even been asked;

b) to respond to aspirations of the heart that have yet to be experienced in a deep way; and

c) to skip those elements which provide the "leverage" by which scripture-Christ-church ministry can be made to come alive.

Since the shift of the mountain called Christianity, a whole new sub-atomic world of ministry has opened up beneath our feet. To ignore it is to risk irrelevance and to court incomprehension. To acknowledge it is to set the stage for a vibrant ministry of good news, for *the whole good news of Christianity is God's response to the primal cry for help.*

God's response is an unfolding one: first, in terms of scripture (Step 5), then in terms of Christ (Step 6), and then in terms of Christ among us, church (Steps 7-9).

Imagine the good news of scripture, Christ and church as three diamonds. For centuries we have been looking at one side of these diamonds. Let us now slowly turn these diamonds around. Without forgetting the beauty of the traditional side, let us see if we can discover that the good news of scripture, Christ and church is even greater than we thought it was. The great mystery and splendor of the gospel is that the good news is always "good-er" than you think it is.

And so, to the scripture diamond. . . .

[1]Jean Danielou, *The Scandal of Truth,* Helicon Press, 1962, p.

8
BIBLE, ANYONE?

Scripture as Matchmaker (Step 5)

One of Saint Paul's adventures that didn't get into the *Acts of the Apostles* happened on his second missionary journey. Sitting on the deck of his ship, he was reviewing his notes on the oral gospel and gazing at an island in the distance. Suddenly a huge wave hit the ship, and knocked the notes out of his hand and overboard. Fortunately, the apostle had a set of xerox copies in his room below deck, so he quickly forgot the whole incident.

On his third missionary journey, Paul visits the island that he passed that day. Racing down the gangplank, he hops a taxi for the center of town. He stands up in the market place and announces, "Have I got good news! Have I got gospel for you!" When he has the crowd's attention, he proceeds to tell them the gospel story. At first everyone is eager, excited and attentive. Gradually, however, some begin to yawn, others are looking around, and some start slipping away. Finally, one little fellow raises his hand and says, "Mr. Paul, we admire your enthusiasm. You certainly get excited about this material. But we have a problem. We know all these stories. They washed up on the beach a few years ago; someone mimeographed them and passed them around. Now here's our problem: ABC, CBS and NBC give us something new every night. The libraries give us new novels to read. The newspapers give us new stories every day. Do you have anything new? If it's only going to be S.O.S. — the same old stuff — thanks, but no thanks."

The moral of the story is: The good news is not good news just because it's good. It has to be not only good but *new*. This is what plagues our ministry. "Listen to these stories, they're good for you," we proclaim. "But I've heard them a hundred times," they retort. "Jesus rose from the dead. Great. You told me that last Easter. What are you going to tell me this Easter?"

Scripture as Encounter Causer

How do we make the good news new? Do we make up new stories? Hardly. But we can try a new approach to scripture. For the most part we have been using it as a source of religious information. This is one good way of unleashing its power, by telling us about God, about ourselves, about the meaning of life and the deepest aspirations of the human heart. But it's not the only way. There is another, of which many are hardly aware. Scripture can be an *encounter-causer*. It is God's response to the primal cry for help to have love encounters with Him and with others. If we are willing to plunge into the scripture experience, these stories, with God's help, can bring about new love encounters in our lives. Now that is truly new! The television, the novel, the newspaper can tell us new stories, but scripture has a newness all its own: new love encounters in our lives.

How do we use scripture as an encounter-causer? The process is just the opposite of what we do when using it as a source of religious information. Then, we take 20th century people back to the first century: "Isn't it wonderful what Christ said and did for us!" But now we take a first-century event and bring it into the 20th century, by surfacing a corresponding experience between myself and some figure in scripture. Thus the gospel story is not just about some other people long ago and far away but about me, about us, in the here and now.

The Epileptic Boy

An example of a corresponding experience is provided by the story of the father and his epileptic son.[1] Mark speaks of an evil spirit, but the recital of symptoms indicates a classic case of grand mal epilepsy. In those days of minimum medical and scientific knowledge, anything not understood was assigned to preternatural causes. The father is trying to care for his physically handicapped son without any of the helps that today's knowledge of epilepsy and medical progress have provided. He is also fighting a psychological battle. In those days, and even today in some places, a moral stigma is attached to physical suffering. "That is a wicked family. There must be sin, perhaps by the parents, perhaps by the boy himself, for such a thing to occur." The father finally builds up enough courage to seek out Jesus and ask him to cure his son. As luck would have it, Jesus is not there. The disciples try to help, and fail. Nothing happens in the Middle East unless it happens in a crowd, so half the neighborhood is there. And now the neighbors are doubly convinced that it is a wicked family.

Jesus arrives on the scene and at the same time the boy experiences a seizure. Jesus appears to be aloof. He engages the father in a recital of the case history as if he were filling out a medical form: in the past the boy has rolled into a fire, he has nearly drowned. Finally he asks the father if he believes that he (Jesus) can cure the boy. The father replies, "I do believe; help my unbelief!" What is he really saying? "I'm physically exhausted taking care of my sick son. I'm psychologically exhausted fighting the rash judgment of my neighbors. Your disciples made a fool of me in front of half the town. You engage me in questions as my boy experiences a seizure. I am so worn out that I cannot even begin to believe that you will help me unless you help me to begin to believe."

And Jesus cures the boy. He was not trying to be aloof. He was trying to elicit the primal cry for help.

Now let us put ourselves in the father's shoes. Haven't we all had a corresponding experience? Not identical, or even simi-

lar, but one in which the dynamics are the same. We all know
how the father feels, because we've been there: someone we
love dearly dies; we are in great physical pain; our whole
spiritual life turns to dust; someone we depended on lets us
down in a crisis. Our only prayer is the word "help!" and maybe
we can't even say it.

Where Do You Live?

There are innumerable passages in the gospels that lend
themselves to this kind of analysis. Two young men follow Jesus
hesitantly at the Baptist's bidding and try to get up courage
to introduce themselves.[2] Jesus turns and asks them: "What
are you looking for?" All they can think of to say is "Where do
you live?" and receive the invitation to "come and see." It is
easy to place ourselves in the disciples' shoes. Do we know what
we are looking for? Can we put our finger on just what this
hunger within us is all about, this thirst for a fuller life? Jesus
invites us to visit with him, to come and see where he lives, to
find the fulfillment of our hearts' deepest longings.

The Samaritan woman at the well tries to engage Jesus in
a religious discussion about the location of the true Temple.[3]
He cuts through the verbiage and the disguises and goes to the
heart of her real problem: she has gone through a series of
sexual encounters that have left her dishonest and empty. Far
from resenting his bluntness, she hurries to her neighbors and
urges them to "come and meet a man who has told me everything I ever did." Like the Samaritan woman, we are all sometimes guilty of what Martin Marty calls using religion as a
defense against the radical demands of faith. Like her, we need
someone to break through our defenses and show us what we
are really doing, what we are really like. Not to cast us down,
but to raise us up. We can experience what seems to have
happened to so many people who came in contact with Jesus
of Nazareth. In his presence, they were invited to see themselves as they really were, and to get a glimpse of what they
could be. Some of them seized the opportunity and opened them-

selves to greatness. Some were so enraged at being unmasked
that they did away with him. Most just turned away from a
truth that was too threatening to behold. Are we so different?

One man who wasn't afraid to look and who had the courage
to change was Zaccheus.[4] He must have been dissatisfied with
himself and his life when he climbed that tree. We can only
imagine the rationalizations that he must have indulged in to
preserve his swindler's career and somehow repress the pangs
of guilt. But when face to face with Jesus, he somehow finds
within himself the courage to make a clean break, to give back
all the money, and hear the encomium: "This day salvation has
come to this house." Luke finishes his account here, but of
course the story is not over, and we are invited to write the
closing scene. Maybe salvation came to his house, but first there
must have been a big fight. What did he tell Zelda, his wife,
when he got home that night? How did she take the news of
his conversion? Did she remind him that there was a mortgage
on the house? Honesty is nice, but will it pay the bills? And
what is to become of Irving, their teenage son? He goes to
Jericho Prep, where tuition is 200 drachmas a year. Will he
have to transfer to Jericho High School, where they are busing
in the Samaritan kids? Does any of this sound familiar? Aren't
these the kind of problems we face when we take Jesus too
seriously and decide to be completely honest?

Who's Listening?

When Jesus tells his closest followers that he must go to
Jerusalem to suffer at the hands of his enemies, Peter tries to
talk him out of it.[5] Jesus lashes out at him, calls him a devil
and tells him to get out of his way. Then he lays out the cost
of discipleship: it is nothing less than carrying a cross. We are
told that the disciples "understood none of these things; this
saying was hid from them, and they did not grasp what was
said."[6] Of course, *we* understand. Or do we? Do we really accept
his terms, or do we hope to work out some kind of deal? Maybe
a small cross, or a more comfortable one? His words, when we
really listen to them, are just as blunt and uncompromising,

just as hard to accept as the first time he said them at Caesarea Philippi. And if we are as dense as the disciples, it is probably for the same reason: when they stopped listening to talk of suffering and death, they failed to hear what he said about resurrection.

Pontius Pilate really didn't want to execute anybody. He just wanted everyone to give in a little, to be reasonable, so he could work out a settlement where there would be something for everybody.[7] The way he saw it, what he had here was a failure to communicate. He wanted to be fair, but not *too* fair; otherwise it could damage his career. These Jews were so damned stubborn, and this Jesus wasn't giving him any help. What does he expect — a hundred percent justice? Doesn't he know that governors have to keep a lot of people happy? Today, anyone who cannot identify with Pilate is probably very short on self-knowledge. We are all born compromisers, and we have all become experts in rationalization and self-deception. We all know what it is to be tempted to wash our hands when we should take a stand.

Time Delay

The surfacing of the corresponding experience leads to the genesis of encounter with God and others. We have noticed an interesting thing when using scripture as an encounter-causer. Many times the actual encounter — between the person and Christ, between the person and others — does not take place during the reading or hearing of the scripture but a day, a week, or a month later. It is a kind of time bomb effect. Over the years we have inadvertently been conditioned to expect an immediate effect from scripture. For example, we listen to the readings and the homily at Mass in hopes of an immediate insight, challenge, or grace. Sometimes it happens. If it doesn't . . . "I didn't get anything out of it." Without realizing it we have boxed the power of God's word into twenty-minute containers. With the time bomb effect of scripture as an encounter-causer, its power is unleashed. It goes on 24 hours a day, seven days a week. The encounter can take place at any time.

*   *   *

When the gospels were being formed, what was the primary goal? It was certainly not to impart maximum religious information. If that was what the evangelists had in mind, they didn't do a very good job. The gospels will never win any prizes either as extensive biographies of Christ or as histories of the early church. Their primary goal was to tell the Jesus story in such a way that others might have the same encounter experiences as those who were part of the story. They wanted people to experience encounters with Christ, or with others in the presence of Christ, the way they had. That is why the gospels were so long in forming, first in oral form, and then in written (and re-written) versions. The creation of an encounter-causer ministerial instrument takes a lot of time.

In the early church, the gospels were used primarily as encounter-causers and only secondarily as sources of religious information. Down through the centuries, the focus gradually changed as more and more people entered the church not by adult conversions but by birth. The ministerial question now becomes how best to share our Christian heritage with our children. So gradually the secondary goal of information became primary and the primary goal was lost sight of or retreated into the background.

In proposing scripture as an encounter-causer, we are not introducing something very, very new. Rather, in some small way we are contributing to the rediscovery of something very, very old. In using scripture in this manner, we begin to meet Christ in a new way.

[1]Mark 9:14-27.

[2]John 1:35-45.

[3]John 4:4-32.

[4]Luke 19:1-10.

[5]Matthew16:21-28.

[6]Luke 18:34.

[7]John 18:33 — 19:16

9
HEEEEEEEERE'S JESUS!

Caring Enough to Send the Very Best (Step 6)

Before the quantum leap changed our religious world forever, the question for ministry concerning the Incarnation was *how*. How can Jesus be both human and divine? Although that is still a very important question, the shift of the mountain has moved another concern to front and center. The prime ministerial question now is *why*. Why did God come among us in the flesh? If we don't have a good motivating answer to that question, the good news of incarnation will fall on deaf ears.

Why did Jesus come among us? The traditional answer is to save us from sin. Now that's true and wonderful, but it isn't the whole truth or the full wonder. Of course he came to liberate us from sin. But you can't just have liberation *from* something; you must also have liberation *for* something. Jesus came to free us *from* sin *for* encounter. Deliverance from sin is still immensely important, because sin is such an obstacle to love encounter with God and others. Many people suspect that sin is wrong because it's fun: big fun, big sin; little fun, little sin. Yet sin is not wrong because it is enjoyable or convenient or satisfying. It is wrong because it cripples our potential for encounter with God or with others, and contributes to the disorientation of our true selves.

Why did God come among us? Jesus came for two reasons:

    1) to encounter you personally;

    2) to enable you to encounter others.

So Christ becomes *the* Encounter Causer. Scripture the encounter causer gradually introduces us to Christ the Encounter Causer.

To Encounter You Personally

What do we mean when we say that Christ wants to encounter you personally? What do we mean when we say that Jesus saves? What are the full implications of salvation?

Jesus came to liberate you from all the minus factors in your life and to enhance the plus factors beyond your wildest dreams.

As regards the minus factors, Jesus came to liberate you from the disorientation of sin, the greatest obstacle to the meaning of life. But he also came to deliver you from all the minus factors that come in the wake of sin — loneliness, deprivation, injury, disease, ennui, aimlessness, injustice, death . . . the list is endless. Christ's ultimate purpose is to destroy all of these, even your death by your personal resurrection. But for now we live in a mysterious, unfolding world where these minus factors diminish but refuse to disappear. There are times, as in a terminal illness, when even this does not happen. That's when Christ says: "Give me half. You are not alone; we are in this together."[1]

We are dealing with a great mystery here. Paradoxically, it is sometimes in the midst of intense strife and deep despair that unbelievable encounters with God and others can occur. The answer to the problem of suffering is, in a way, very easy: God draws good from evil. Yet the textbook answer rings hollow and means little or nothing at all when great suffering comes upon us. Maybe all we can do at a time like that is reach for

the hand of an incarnate God who took on the human condition
and underwent attack, pain, character assassination and execution. We must not lose sight, however, of the fact that Christ's
ultimate goal is to destroy utterly all our minus factors. Until
then, if we are open, remarkable things can happen to us in
the here and now.

If Jesus came to liberate us *from* the minus factors, he also
came to dispose us *for* the plus factors. And this brings us back
to the basic heart wishes: to love, to be loved, to share, to
blossom out. The most profound questions of meaning are waiting to be answered, the deepest longings of our hearts are
waiting to be fulfilled. The possibilities here are unbounded. If
we are open, the possible experiences are beyond all calculation.
The deeper our basic heart wishes, the more intense the search
for meaning and the primal cry for more, the greater the experiences can become. This is a recurring theme in the New Testament. Three examples of this theme are the cure of the blind,
the healing of the paralytic, and the multiplication of the loaves.

The Cure of the Blind

Several times in the gospel narratives we read of Jesus giving
sight to the blind. The meaning of these marvelous cures seems
at first sight to be obvious: Jesus felt sorry for the people and
did what we all wish we could do — restore their sight. On one
level this is true. Jesus had compassion on those who suffered
physical maladies, and he used his power to heal them. But
there is a deeper meaning here, and the author of John's Gospel
brings it out: "I am the light of the world. Whoever follows me
will have the light of life and will never walk in darkness."[2]

When we see a blind person tapping along the streets with
a cane, what thoughts run through our minds? We feel sorry
for the person, of course. Perhaps we admire their courage in
venturing out in the streets. We may feel a bit ashamed of
complaining about our troubles, which pale in comparison.
Whatever our reactions, they usually come down to saying, in
one way or another, that the blind person has a terrible affliction

and that we are glad that we can see. But of course there is more than one kind of blindness. There is blindness that does not afflict the physical organs but which keeps people from seeing what is really important, what is worth striving for . . . even what life is all about. There is a blindness of the heart, which closes us to all considerations except those which serve our narrow self-interest. We are all, at one time or another, blind in ways like these.

Jesus wants to cure us of this blindness, and he can if we let him. As a sign of his willingness and his power to heal us, he cures the blind man. This is an example of the unbounded possibilities that are open to us if we expand our heart wishes and let his power work within us.

The Healing of the Paralytic

Another case of Jesus using his healing power to point to a deeper reality is that of the paralyzed man.[3] When the man has been lowered through the roof by his friends and lies before Jesus, he hopes that his body will be cured. Instead he hears the words, "Your sins are forgiven." A beautiful thought, but not exactly what they had in mind!

Jesus deflects our attention from the man's physical malady, not because he doesn't take the body's ills seriously, but because he is playing for higher stakes. There is a kind of paralysis which is worse than that which afflicts the limbs. It is paralysis of the heart, and it takes many forms: greed, cruelty, selfishness, insensitivity, dishonesty, just to name a few. We have a word to cover them all — Sin. It does not make the same impact on us as the sight of a man who cannot walk or use his arms. But in its most virulent forms it is far more deadly, and it can cripple us without our even being aware of it.

Jesus has compassion on the crippled man in front of him and cures him. But he reminds us of the paralysis that we all carry within us, and offers to make us whole again. In other words, he encourages us to aspire to health not only of the body but also of the spirit. And his cure of the paralytic is a sign

that he can do it. "I will prove to you, then, that the Son of
Man has authority on earth to forgive sins. . . . I tell you, get
up, pick up your mat, and go home!"

The Multiplication of the Loaves

By now we detect a pattern in Jesus' ministry. He begins
with basic human needs of which we are all conscious and
whose urgency is evident to all — the need for physical health,
the need to see — and points to deeper needs of which we are
not always aware but, which are no less urgent. A striking
example of this pedagogy is the multiplication of the loaves.[4]
As the incident is related in the gospels, the need for food was
hardly a critical one. The crowd would go hungry for a while,
but presumably they would all get a late supper. It is in John's
gospel that the meaning and intent of the miracle is made clear.
The next day, in the synagogue at Capharnaum, Jesus bluntly
reminds the people of why they are present: yesterday he filled
their bellies with free food: "You are looking for me because
you ate the bread and had all you wanted."[5] He tries to make
them (and us) see that there is a hunger within all of us that
no amount of ordinary bread will ever satisfy. That kind of food
fills us for a while, but soon leaves us hungry again; and it
does not even touch this other, deeper hunger. "Do not work
for the food that spoils; instead, work for the food that lasts
for eternal life."[6]

This food, of course, is the Eucharist. It is not the food that
is usually on people's minds; most of them feel they can do
quite well without it. For them, the search for ordinary bread
is more than enough to occupy their striving and satisfy their
aspirations. But only the bread that Jesus offers us can satisfy
our longing for the infinite, for the fullness of life. Like those
first people that God fed in the desert, ordinary bread will take
us just so far: "Your ancestors ate manna in the desert, but
they died. But the bread that comes down from heaven is of
such a kind that whoever eats it will not die. I am the living
bread that came down from heaven. If anyone eats this bread,
he will live forever."[7]

To Encounter You Personally: Justice

The encounters we have been describing are intensely personal. In them we meet Jesus one-on-one, as he calls each one of us by name. And yet this is not to imply that our relationship with him is meant to be purely individualistic. We are all in this together; there is a social dimension implicit even in the most intimate relationship with Christ. He calls us not to withdraw from the world but to share responsibility for it. We cannot respond to him by shutting ourselves off from others. By the same token, we cannot attain our individual potential while our communities are victimized by political, economic, social or religious injustice.[8]

A quick look around the world reveals not only individuals and groups but even whole systems often acting in direct opposition to the purpose of Christ. When we analyze these systems more closely, the amount of systemic violence (political, economic, social and even religious) is overwhelming.

The greatest protection of one of these systems is the fact that it *is*. Over the centuries we have developed a fine nose for uncovering personal sin. But in our concentration on the microcosm of the individual, we have all but overlooked the macrocosm of the system. A single murder grabs the headlines. The murder of thousands to insure the continuance of an unjust system rates a small article on page five or, worse yet, no notice at all. People, especially those at the traditional level of faith value appropriation, tend to assume that if a system *is*, it is *good*. They will admit, of course, that because of the human element mistakes will be made. But they find it hard to conceive that the system itself could be wrong, preserving injustice and its own existence by its very internal structure.

Jesus came to liberate the world from all unjust systems. He undertook to do this by his preaching of the Kingdom and got himself killed in the process as he clashed with the power systems of his day. Kingdom used to be regarded as a completely other-worldly reality which constituted the reward for a life of individual justice. Theologians today are making it clear that the Kingdom is *now*, though not the fullness of Kingdom which, of course, coincides with the fullness of time. It is a constantly growing process within our midst. And herein lies the rub. Christ came not only to liberate us but to empower us to liberate one another. If we neglect Christ's call to Kingdom and turn a blind eye to systemic injustice — political, economic,, social or religious — the coming of God's reign is postponed and the words of the Lord's prayer, "thy kingdom come," ring hollow.

All of us, at one time or another, have frozen on hearing news of some accident or tragedy. We froze because the circumstances of the event had a familiar ring to them and we feared someone we knew might be involved. A sigh of relief came forth when we learned that it was not our friends but other people. It's a natural reaction and easily understood. Yet Christ came to teach us that there are no "other people." There are no strangers in the world, just brothers and sisters, all of whom are meant to share in the kingdom. Systemic injustice visited upon "other people" different from us by life's circumstances or separated by geography tends to be beyond the scope of our psychic search-light. Yet this is what Christ's kingdom is all about. If we are not part of the solution, we are part of the problem.

To Enable You to Encounter Others

Jesus came among us to heat up the chemistry of human encounter. Christ the Encounter Causer increases your ability to love beyond what human logic says you should have. You become a kind of bionic lover. Not only is your ability to love increased, but it rides a psychic searchlight that extends ever farther out until finally it encompasses the whole of Kingdom reality — all "other people."

Christ not only increases your ability to love, he increases your ability to be loved. He enhances your attractiveness to others so that they are drawn to you beyond what any human logic would call for.

Christ the Encounter Causer is the cornerstone of all community: friendship, family, parish, religious group, justice endeavor. It all begins to fall apart if Christ is not present; conversely, when we allow Christ's influence to work upon us, the potential is unlimited.

Christ's life culminates in the cosmic event called Easter-Pentecost. But he has not gone away. He is among us in church.

[1]Notice here the echoes of the working description of love, p. 40 .

[2]John 8:12.

[3]Mark 2:1-12.

[4]John 6:1-14.

[5]v. 26.

[6]v. 27.

[7]vv. 49-51.

[8]Cf. p. 41 .

10
WHERE IS JESUS NOW?

Alive and Well and in Church (Steps 7-9)

Christ has not gone. He is among us in church. So far, so good. But what is church? And what is Christ doing in it?

Just as a further examination of the diamond of scripture revealed to us not only scripture as religious information but also scripture as encounter-causer,

Just as further examination of the Christ diamond opened up to us a Christ who not only frees us from sin but also liberates us for encounter,

So now it becomes necessary to probe the church diamond for deeper insights into church.

If with the quantum leap in Christianity today it becomes a ministerial imperative to make the good news new,

If our ministry demands that we respond not only to the *how* of Incarnation but also to the *why,*

So now it becomes a ministerial imperative — the most crucial of all — to uncover deeper insights into what is church.

How do we probe for these deeper insights?

Just as scripture the encounter causer introduced us to Christ *the* Encounter Causer,

So the culmination of Christ's life, Easter-Pentecost, will be the key to deeper insight into what is church.

Unfortunately, many people look upon church as a kind of spiritual General Motors, a sacred multinational with friendly offices in every neighborhood which dispenses pious ceremonies at particular moments in our lives. We know church is more than that, but what is it? For a clue, let us turn to Easter-Pentecost.

Easter

What is the fullness of the good news of Easter? Of course it means Jesus rose from the dead with an immortal body, but it implies so much more. Let us go back for a moment to Step Two of the Christian Discovery Process.[1] Here we investigated the basic heart wishes — to love, to be loved, to share and to blossom out. Easter means that Christ attained an infinite fulfillment of the basic heart wishes. If you want to begin to comprehend the full implications of Easter, go deep into your heart, take every desire, hope, and longing that you have, and start to extend them to infinity. In doing so, you will begin to get a glimpse of what Easter is all about.

There is something in most of us that resists this kind of effort. We are so at home with the work-a-day, prosaic, humdrum world of the present that we are uncomfortable with anything that smacks of the visionary. To us is addressed the Japanese proverb, "The frog in the well thinks it is at the center of the world." Ministry in these changing times demands that we get out of the well and expand our mini-minds and mini-hearts. We have to have the courage to think new thoughts. If we don't expand both thought and aspiration, we tend to collapse back upon ourselves, to implode. The ultimate implosion in the universe may well be the theoretical black hole from which no light shines forth. Let those in ministry beware!

But what is it that will help us to break out of the restrictive little boxes in our minds and hearts and initiate our probe? The answer is . . .

Pentecost

What is the fullness of the good news of Pentecost? Of course it means wind, tongues of fire, charism and conversion, but it encompasses even more than that. It means that what Christ has attained — the infinite fulfillment of the basic heart wishes — he shares with us to an unbelievable extent *in the here and now*. Of course, an infinity of this must wait until we have gone through the evolutionary transition called death-and-resurrection. But a foretaste beyond all imagining is possible in our immediate future, which begins today.

To understand what this means in more down-to-earth terms, consider the disciples who experienced the first Pentecost as described in the Acts of the Apostles. What happens to them? They are inspired and transformed, of course; thousands are converted, and the church is born. But what do they do? How are their lives changed? What are the palpable signs of their new life in the Spirit?

> All the believers continued together in close fellowship and shared their belongings with one another. They would sell their property and possessions, and distribute the money among all, according to what each one needed. Day after day they met as a group in the Temple, and they had their meals together in their homes, eating with glad and humble hearts, praising God and enjoying the good will of all the people. . . .
>
> The group of believers was one in mind and heart. . . . With great power the apostles gave witness to the resurrection of the Lord Jesus, and God poured

rich blessings on them all. There was no one in the group who was in need.[2]

If we read between the lines of this idealized description of the first Christian community, we see people caring for one another, sharing a common vision and a deep down joy. They are not spared the thousand natural shocks that flesh is heir to, but they have inner resources to help deal with them and not be vanquished by them. Their security comes not from the accumulation of possessions and signs of status, but from a consciousness of being loved by God and by one another. Their whole scale of values is altered; they have a sense of what is really important. They are in touch with life. They see others not as rivals or enemies to be outdone or outflanked, but as members of a family committed to their common welfare. They are not turned in on themselves, jealously guarding their turf; they are already moving outward, spreading the Good News and offering to share their new life with anyone who will listen. They are men and women for others, and in this way most of all they resemble Christ.

When we compare the church as we experience it to this first community as portrayed in the New Testament, we may become discouraged and judge too quickly that we have failed completely to live up to the ideal they set before us. But a closer look at the limited, sinful people who make up the Body of Christ reveals more of a likeness than first meets the eye. We do try to care for one another in many ways that may be taken for granted but do not escape the notice of Him whose grace makes it possible. Every moment of every day, people respond to the needs of those around them and far away. Sometimes they consciously advert to the person of Christ in those they serve, more often they do not. But love is shown, as people go out of themselves in a thousand generous and quietly heroic ways. This is the Pentecost process happening here and now, as the members of Christ's body, vitalized by the Spirit's action, give the world a foretaste of Omega-Kingdom. They are a kind of model city, a "coming attraction" of the fullness of life that awaits us.

Friedrich Nietzche once said that Christians could not possibly believe what they assert, otherwise they could not go about with such long faces. He reminds us that if Christ is really risen and his Spirit really at work in the world, then someone must be alive in a new way. The good things that happen in church are signs that Christ indeed lives and reigns in a suffering and unfinished world.

Church

Now we are ready to address the question: "What is church?"

Church is the risen Christ

> Among the People of God

>> Doing Easter-Pentecost Process.

But the good news of church is better still. Not only does Christ do Easter-Pentecost process; he empowers frail humans to do it to each other. And so . . . .

Church is the risen Christ

> Among/with the People of God

> Doing Easter-Pentecost Process.

*   *   *

Step 7 of the Christian Discovery Process encompasses an *initial* new insight and experience of what it means to be a baptized Christian. Step 8 is a *filling out* of the implications of Christian activity. Step 9 is, of course, the *open-ended possibilities* of Christian life. It has infinite potential and can blossom out in a limitless variety of ways. Step 9 also has, paradoxically, within it the seeds of beginning anew. Once again the person moves from where he or she is (Step 1) to become a searching person (Step 2). The Christian Discovery Process is not a once-only experience. It can go on for a life time as we strive for ever higher levels of faith appropriation and union with Christ and others.

Let us now begin to examine the implications of church as Easter-Pentecost Process.

[1]Pp. 38-42

[2]Acts 2:44-47, 4:32-34.

11
What Kind of Church?

Forward to Basics (Steps 7-9 cont'd)

In this time of quantum leap within Christianity, how can the people of God best cooperate with the risen Christ in the accomplishment of Easter-Pentecost Process? The challenge is to participate in many deep-seated changes. Cosmetic corrections will not suffice for an Exodus generation. At least four fundamental shifts must take place within the church:

1. From static mindset to process mindset;

2. From centripetal church to centrifugal church;

3. From a descending church to an ascending/descending church;

4. From domesticated Gospel to Gospel as agent of change.

Let us examine each of these in turn.

From static mindset to process mindset

The static mindset looks at the world and sees it is *imperfect*. No one will argue with that; a quick glance at the newspaper tells us that life has been rendered imperfect by sin and human failure. This mindset, however, sees the world as *complete*. It is as if God has created an already finished world, and our only task is to remove any imperfections that remain. Imagine walking into a room and finding all the furniture knocked over and covered with mud. "What does God want us to do?" we ask ourselves. Clean the room, of course, and put it in order.

The process mindset looks at the world, agrees that it is imperfect, but also sees it as *incomplete*. In other words, God is still involved in creation. Creation is not something that happened a long time ago; it is happening now. Not in the sense that God continues to create from nothing, but in the sense that He has a continual plan of development for all creation. We walk into the same room as before and ask, "What does God want us to do?" This time, however, the answer is different. Of course He wants us to clean up the room and put it in order. But He also wants us to make the chairs into better chairs, to improve the tables, the lighting and the ventilation. There is much that remains undone, and it is up to us to decide what has to be done and then to do it.

The static mindset carries with it a basic conviction: that the most important thing in life is to preserve, and the worst thing that can happen is to make a mistake. This conviction resides at an implicit conscious level — at the back of the mind, in the depths of the heart. It colors every opinion the person has and influences every action the person does or fails to do.

The process mindset also carries with it a fundamental conviction: that the most important thing in life is to explore, to probe, to try. The worst thing is not to try. Again, this attitude colors all opinions and decisions.

The static mindset does not allow people to realize that they can change. Imagine an infant who at birth has red contact lenses inserted into her eyes. These are special lenses that require no removal and also adjust to the size of the eye as the baby matures into an adult. As far as she is concerned, the world is red. It is the nature of things.

In like manner, a person wearing static mindset contact lenses observes people operating with a process mindset and becomes convinced that they are violating the nature of things. The minimum reaction is to murmur disapproval. The maximum reaction is to suppress what the others are doing, at all costs. This is to be done under the rubric of purity of doctrine, loyalty, fidelity to tradition, etc.

The irony here is that the Jewish heroes of the Exodus would never have ventured out of the shade of the pyramids and into the desert without a shift to a process mindset. People would not have thrown in their lot with the itinerant missioner called Jesus of Nazareth unless they had the courage to undergo the transformation to process mindset. The same challenges face us.

From centripetal (spiraling-in) church to centrifugal (spiral-out) church

For centuries the church has turned in on itself. It offered a movement away from the world into a safe spiritual haven. The church operated as a fortress, a sanctuary that all were invited to enter. More importantly, it existed for its own sake. The goal of church activity was the furthering of its own power and influence; it had become an end unto itself.

The centrifugal church, on the other hand, spirals out into the world. People are brought into the church so that they may be sent out to serve a world that is not only imperfect but also incomplete.

The church exists not for itself but for the Kingdom. Kingdom used to be conceived as an other-worldly reward for those who lived correctly in the sanctuary called church. The fullness of Kingdom must wait, of course, for the fullness of time, but an unbelievable foretaste is possible here and now.

> Since Jesus was among us to proclaim the Kingdom of God, to realize it here and now, and to demonstrate its meaning by the quality and style of his own life, the Christian seeks to participate in this mission. .

>The human person who is drawn to the Church is
not interested in the cause of the *Church* but in the
cause of the *Kingdom*. The Church is a means to an
end. . . .

>The Church cannot be conceived as a kind of giant
umbrella, under which a segment of mankind hud-
dles to avoid the drenching of a sinful world. Membership in the Church confers a responsibility and a
mission. Apparently, God calls relatively few men to
assume these burdens, and these are not always the
best of people. The Christian community itself is
often the chief stumbling block to the Gospel. But
God calls in spite of this weakness. Indeed, he works
through this weakness, just as he worked through
the weakness of Jesus.[1]

This then is the ultimate purpose of church: not to further
its own institutional strength in a triumphal church, but to
further the coming of Kingdom in all aspects of life — religious,
of course, but also political, economic, and social. The task is
to help people and systems reflect the reign of God. In doing
so, church will recapture the gospel characteristics of leaven,
salt, light on a lampstand.

From descending church to ascending/descending church

We are all familiar with the descending church. Those in
power make a "statement." (The number of possible topics is
infinite). It then becomes the job of the professional theologians
to build up a support theology for the statement. This process
resembles that of the board of directors of a large corporation:
they arrive at a decision and then call in the house lawyers to
draw up the necessary contracts. Those in ministry are to get
all the information out in easily understood terms. The role of
the people is a passive one: to obey orders.

A descending model of church undermines the good news of

Christ's resurrection. It suggests that Jesus is dead and gone, and that the executors of the will must now manage the estate. They have to take Jesus' place.

But if Jesus is risen, then he is alive and well and among the people of God. In an ascending/descending church, the process can begin from below as well as from above. The people live life; they daily try to bring gospel to bear on life and life to bear on gospel. Gospel teachings give insights into life experiences; life experiences bring light to bear on gospel teachings.

None of this is meant to deny the limitations and sinfulness of God's people. Among them are those who make great mistakes, go down blind alleys, and do some downright evil things. But within the people of God there is also the risen Christ. As a result, remarkable things are uncovered in the dialectic, the interaction of gospel and life.

Those in ministry, of course, help people sift out the truly inappropriate from the matrix of life experiences. One of our principal tasks, however, is to be the *poets of the people of God* . . . to help them articulate their life-gospel experiences, to help them write the lyrics and sing their songs. Professional theologians do the same at a more erudite level.

Those in leadership now say, "In light of the life-gospel experiences of God's people, in light of the endeavors of theologians and those in ministry, here is a good model to use." And this model now descends, and the process begins anew, constantly refining and revivifying itself.

From domesticated gospel to gospel as agent of change

Religious consciousness is indeed a strange phenomenon. It can sometimes appropriate a faith system in such a way that the faith system becomes a slave of the status quo. Religion then serves as a cloak of respectability draped over existing structures — political, economic, social, religious — in order not only to legitimize their existence in the present but to insure their perpetuation in the future. Any system protected by a religious cloak has a formidable defense. If someone calls attention to aspects of the system that are inadequate, outmoded or even unjust, that person is accused of attacking religion. This, in turn, justifies the system in attacking the person who raised the question in the first place. Notice that the person is attacked not as a critic of the system but as the enemy of religion. A domesticated gospel provides an almost impenetrable shield. And yet. . . .

And yet, religious consciousness holds in its hands a two-edged sword called the gospel. And if the gospel can be made to swing one way against "enemies" of the system, it can also swing the other way against systemic failure. The system is now forced to undergo scrutiny in the light of gospel imperatives. "Failures" in this context refer not to the shortcomings that derive from human limitations. Those are regrettable but understandable. Rather, "failures" refer to the actual structures within the system that are failing the people they are supposed to serve. The gospel now becomes a change agent. Not change for the sake of change, or as a vehicle for trendiness. If it were just that, the system would have little to fear. Such an ineffectual weapon is easily thrust aside. Rather, the gospel as a change agent *vivifies a gospel people and makes them agents of change.*

The church cannot hope to be a successful force for change in addressing the political, economic, and social injustices of the world unless it is willing to apply the same gospel principles to itself. Unfortunately, religious leaders are prone to apply a double standard of justice and integrity — one for their institutions, and another for the rest of the world. Such hypocrisy is evident to all but those who are so close to it that they cannot see; and it is the occasion of grave scandal. Physicians who refuse to heal themselves soon run out of patients.

The roots of this institutional myopia are sunk deep in the past. In its early existence the church ran up against the Roman Empire whose strength derived from three characteristics: 1) all power was in the hands of a few; 2) only those who were in power decided who got into power; and 3) if push came to shove, the interests of the organization were preferred to the welfare of the members. The strategy of the church, for better or for worse, was to take on the very characteristics of its imperial adversary and beat the enemy at his own game. The Empire crumbled and the church survived, but the question remains: Who won?

For the sake of argument, let us grant that this may have been the best strategy for times past. Perhaps a case could be made that the extremely conservative, even rigid forms of government that the institutional church sometimes assumed were necessary if it was to survive and serve. But given the quantum leap in Christianity today, such a strategy is not only outmoded, it is counterproductive. An empire model of church, resistant to self-criticism and internal reform, is geared to keep people at a level of external faith appropriation. Response to the call of justice and peace comes only when people have reached the level of internal appropriation of faith. And so the gospel as change agent sweeps through the church, challenging it to change its own structures, so that it can in turn be the change agent serving the risen Christ in bringing about the coming of the Kingdom.

The risen Christ helps us in this change. Let us see how.

[1]McBrien, Richard, *Do We Need the Church?*, Harper & Row, 1969, pp. 16, 170-172.

12
WHAT'S HE DOING?

Sacraments as Love Encounters (Steps 7-9 cont'd)

Christ is alive and well and in church. But what is he doing? And how does it affect us?

It should come as a surprise to no one if he were doing the same things now as he did the first time around. After all, he is the same person in his present glorified existence as the young man who walked the roads of Palestine nineteen hundred years ago. But do people think of him this way? To many, the Jesus of History was an appealing figure capable of profound impact on those who saw and heard him and experienced his dynamic, divinity-charged presence. But the Christ of Faith is an airy, unsubstantial being, hard to picture and elusive of human contact. Teenagers call him "abstract."

And yet Jesus did not rise to a new life just so that we could celebrate the memory of his triumph and contemplate him in his glory. Life is ordered to activity. Jesus conquered death not just to "open the gates of heaven" for us to pass through later on after we die. He wants to share that life with us *now*. And he does so, if we let him, in much the same way that is described in the New Testament.

Many Christians have the inarticulate notion that Jesus once did many marvelous things to other people in other places a long time ago, but does not do them any more. He taught the people, forgave sinners, healed the sick and raised the dead. How exciting it must have been to be alive then and to witness his great deeds! Of course that sort of thing does not go on today. But fortunately we have a written record of his words and deeds and can recall them for our edification and inspiration.

This inadequate grasp of Jesus' life and mission relegates him to a first-century existence that is remote from us and fails to touch us in our down-to-earth, everyday lives. But of course he didn't settle for that. He wants to enlighten and inspire us. When we hurt, he wants to heal us. When we fall, he wants to raise us up. And he can do all this and more in the love encounters that we call sacraments. In Baptism and Confirmation he raises us to new life and gives us his Spirit. In the Eucharist, he feeds us with the bread of life, his own body and blood. In Penance, he heals the ravages of sin. In the sacrament of Anointing, he offers healing of soul and body and entry to a new and fuller life.

To the casual observer, it may seem that all the really exciting things happened to those who knew Jesus in the flesh, and that we have only the leftovers, pale imitations of the real thing. But with the discerning eyes of faith we can see that it is just the opposite. The events related in the gospels, spectacular as they are, are really only coming attractions. The evangelist call them "signs" — striking gestures pointing to realities far more significant, at a much deeper level. The people he cured on the streets of Jerusalem got sick again, but the healing he offers us is an enduring return to full health. The people who ate the loaves and fish on the hillside in Galilee became hungry again, but we are assured that if we partake of the Eucharist we need never go hungry again (Jn 6:35). The widow's son and Lazarus were raised to life, but they grew sick again and died; we are promised a life stronger even than death.

He does all this not just for us individually, but so that we may in turn share that life with others and so build up the body of Christ. The Jesus of History not only touched people's lives and changed them, but also made them agents of change. He can do the same for us if we open ourselves to him. As we have all seen, social activism often fails to have an impact on people and institutions commensurate with the zeal and energy expended. In the sacramental life of the church there is available the strength we need if we are to make a lasting difference in the struggle for justice and peace.

Pardon us for a few moments while we beat a dead horse. There is a kind of pseudotheology of sacrament which still lingers in the popular mind, which may be called the conduit theory. According to this theory, grace is a colorless, gaseous liquid which flows only through prescribed conduits known as sacraments. The latter are moments of magic preferably removed from the stream of daily life. The recipients are primarily passive, and need only to plug into the prescribed conduit. They can then gas up on sanctifying grace which lodges somewhere in the chest area. Also available are certain emanations invisible to the human eye but rumored to be long and narrow rays (actual graces) which push us through life with a particular focus on good deeds.

So much for how *not* to present sacraments. But how should we unfold them? Many ways are possible, of course, but here is an orientation that offers some interesting possibilities.

The sacraments may be presented as *love encounters* (with Christ and others) within the Easter-Pentecost process. The way to make each sacrament come alive is to ask the questions:

— How does this love encounter respond to the basic heart wishes?

— How does it resonate with our deepest longings?

— What intimations does it offer of the ultimate union that awaits us in the fullness of time?

Each sacrament has its own "personality" and unfolds according to its own dynamics. Let us consider a few brief examples from some of the sacraments.

Baptism

In virtue of your baptism, Christ plunges daily into your life and says to you: "Your heart wishes are my heart wishes. Let us work together to attain them. Your sorrows are mine; let us try to overcome them. If nothing else, give me half. You are not alone. Even in the ordinary, prosaic activities of life like waiting for a bus or watching television, I find it an adventure to be with you."

If Christ plunges into your life, then you also plunge into his. In virtue of your baptism and incorporation into Christ, you preached the Sermon on the Mount, had compassion on the leper, challenged the authorities, were terrified in Gethsemani, triumphed on Easter morning. This is not theological poetic license but reality. Even though Christ's actions took place nineteen hundred years ago in the Middle East, we are dealing with a *risen* Christ who is both trans-temporal and trans-geographical. All time and space are his. We cannot impose our space-time limitations on a risen Christ, so he renders his experiences and your reality as one.

To experience what it means to be a baptized Christian, pick up the gospels and read them as your biography. Every place it says "Jesus" insert your own name. Every place it says *he, his* or *him,* insert *I, my, me.* See if you do not get new insights into the union of Christ's life and yours. More importantly, see if you do not hear encounter time bombs ticking.

One of the authors had the privilege, a few years ago, of talking to a Korean priest who had been jailed for eight months for speaking out on justice and peace. On hearing the above, he exclaimed, "That's how I experienced the gospels in jail. What was happening to me and what had happened to Christ was all one. It was all *I.*" Most of us will not go to jail, but this kind of identification with Christ is possible for all of us.

By Baptism Christ enhances the chemistry of human encounter in your life. Both your ability to love and your ability to be loved are intensified. Christ's gospel ministry has become part of your life, and your life now becomes an extension of Christ's ministry to others. By Baptism Christ empowers you for ministry. The gospel continues!

Confirmation

The Spirit received in Confirmation opens up new possibilities of prayer, which becomes an encounter not only with God but also with those whom you love but who are at a distance. Missioners know this at first hand, for half the people they love are always on the other side of the globe. But whether the distance is ten thousand miles or ten city blocks, the problem is the same: separation. The Spirit enables you to overcome the separation so that prayer, while being an encounter with Christ, also becomes an intimate, highly personal encounter with others. A whole new dimension of prayer opens up.

It is important not to get caught up in the mechanics or mathematics of such prayer. Some questions are distracting and sterile: Who is stage center in my consciousness — Christ or others? Is Christ getting prime time? Are my friends each getting equal time? To succumb to these questions is to bring the whole process to a screeching halt. The Spirit sees to it that wherever Christ is in your consciousness, that is stage center. The Spirit is a God for whom one day is as a thousand years and a thousand years is as one day. The Spirit does not schedule peak moments with a stopwatch.

The psychic searchlight of encounter prayer begins to extend out ever more. More and more people are included — especially those in need of love, in need of justice and hence in need of your ministry. As the scope of your encounter prayer is widened, so the Spirit of the risen Christ extends your ministerial efforts. As Baptism, so also Confirmation empowers you for ministry.

Eucharist

Once again, only in more dramatic fashion, the risen Christ enables you to break out of the confines of your space-time limitations. As the symbols of our daily lives, bread and wine, become the Body and Blood of the risen Christ, unbelievable encounter possibilities arise in the Mass event. Once again, only with more immediacy and intimacy because of the instrumentality of Christ's risen body in the Eucharist, you plunge into his life and he plunges into yours.

In like manner, the joys and sorrows and ordinary events that make up your life reality become one with the sorrows and joys and ordinary life experiences of others. This is especially true of those around the world who are in need of justice and peace. Their life realities now become part of your life!

There are no strangers
    in the world.
Only brothers and sisters
Who are in prison
    in Korea or Chile,
Who suffer malnutrition
    and work in a sweatshop
    in Africa or India,
Who are killed
    in Latin America.

Their lives become a part of your life. But in the Eucharist the risen Christ can enable you to experience even greater intimacy. You *become* those people:

I am in prison
    in Korea or Chile.
I suffer malnutrition
    while working in a sweatshop
    in Africa or India.
I am being killed
    in Latin America.

Thus social justice flows from the Eucharist and is at the very core of Christianity. But ask most people what is at the center of their Christian faith and they will reply, "Jesus is God. Keep the commandments. Go to church." "And where is social justice?" you ask. "Well, you see, there's a shelf off to the side. On it are ten nice optional things, including justice and peace, that you may do as a Christian: Pick any two. Justice doesn't happen to be one of my choices. . . . Actually, those who do pick it make me rather nervous." It's not that people are *against* social justice; they're just not *for* it. But an openness to Christ the encounter causer in the Eucharist can bring social justice from the shelf to a place at the core of Christian existence. Thus Christ extends the scope of your ministry. As Baptism and Confirmation, so also Eucharist empowers you for ministry.

*   *   *

The sacraments are not isolated realities, serving as mere ends in themselves. They empower people for ministry, for community building, for the inbreaking of the Kingdom. They call our attention to the fact that all life experiences are holy things. They point out the sacramentality of all of human life.

And so you enter all aspects of life to do ministry. But who are you?

13
Who Are You?

More than You Ever Dreamed (Step 10)

At the start of this book, we said that if you want to do ministry well, you "have to know the territory" — the people you serve, the religious and cultural context within which you and they work and live. To help them find their best selves, you must also know who you are. This is true in all generations, but even more so in an Exodus Generation, a time of quantum leap. Your task is to help others discover the fullness of life, so you are an *enabler*. But you also have to share the experience with the people you serve, so you are a *co-seeker*. Because there is always a deeper appropriation of faith to be achieved, and a closer union with Christ and others to be discovered, you are never above the process.

At present we are all in a jungle called Life in a clearing called Now. People are huddling together and asking, "What do we do? Which way do we go?" You raise your hand and say, "There is a path through this jungle. It's called 'gospel' or 'Christian discovery.' I know something about the path and hope to help you find it. But I'll have to go with you, because I'm looking, too."

Before the recent quantum leap in Christianity, most ministerial relationships were vertical. "I know the catechism and you don't." "I know theology and you don't." "I'm a Christian and you're not." In a world of external faith appropriation, this presented no problem. But once the mountain called Christianity shifts, people begin to resent always being at the bottom of vertical relationships with those in ministry. The resentment soon turns to resistance, and a lot of ministerial effort comes to naught. The great irony is that it is not your ministerial efforts that are being resisted but the ministerial relationship itself.

If you remember that you are a co-seeker as well as an enabler, you will be comfortable with horizontal relationships in your ministry. This is not to suggest a purely egalitarian situation. Because of your role as enabler, a vertical relationship exists. Because you are also a co-seeker, a horizontal — and potentially very fruitful — relationship also exists between you and those you serve.

No More Business as Usual

How important is it for those in ministry to adopt these new attitudes, to accept the status of co-seeker? Serious studies of the American religious scene indicate that failure to do so may alienate large numbers of active and potential church members, and will certainly erode the influence of religious leadership on the beliefs, values and behavior of the people we are trying to reach. Consider this report from Dr. William J. McCready, program director of the National Opinion Research Center at the University of Chicago:

> Religious faith remains strong, Dr. McCready said, but for growing numbers of people an individual search for meaning has become the central religious experience, replacing unquestioning obedience to religious authority.
>
> "This transition is not from authority to anarchy but to conscience," he said. "For many people it is an uncomfortable, messy transition."[1]

We may be tempted to interpret these findings as simply the latest mix of bad and good news, and try to do business as usual. To do so will be to ignore just how deep this current runs, how radical a shift has occurred. It shows up not only in the way people search for meaning and express belief, but also in the way they make moral decisions.

> Many surveys have shown a declining influence of religious authorities on behavior. Dr. McCready said that because Americans had been powerfully imbued with the values of freedom and conscience, the pattern would probably continue.
>
> "Americans don't respond to moral imperatives," he said. "They increasingly behave any way they want to. They've been told to trust their consciences, and that's what they're doing."[2]

The conclusion is inescapable. People in increasing numbers are not going to listen to religious leaders who tell them, in effect, that the religious and moral search has been completed by others, and that they need only to follow those in the know. They need guides who will humbly join them in the search.

Christ the Seeker

People in ministry have always experienced an affinity with Christ in their role as enabler. Christ was the great evangelizer, and in our own way each of us tries to emulate him. Yet when it comes to our own spiritual search, that affinity is often lacking. "After all, Jesus was God and I'm only human."

Now the Incarnation is a mystery, and we do not pretend to solve completely the problem of the human consciousness of Christ. But isn't it strange that people who can deal with a Jesus who experienced hunger, pain, fear and even death, find it difficult to relate to a Jesus who had to probe and search in a human way?

Jesus was not born with a copy of the New Testament in his

hip pocket. Look carefully amidst the straw in the crib: no copy of the gospels. Check out the videotapes of the Sermon on the Mount: no Jesus reading from Part Two of the bible. He wasn't God just dressed up like a man. He didn't merely role-play at being human. So where did he get the Good News? He attained it by seeking. Like each of us, Jesus had to probe, search, try things out, select, reject, try again and keep on praying. And in so doing he gradually arrived at his message of the kingdom.

It was not an arbitrarily chosen day that Jesus put down his carpenter's tools and went on the road as an itinerant missioner. He set out when his own grasp of the good news was firm enough that he felt a confidence — and an urgency — to share it. Throughout his ministry the search continued, as he kept plumbing the depths of his message which, in turn, he then shared with others. The search reached its completion in resurrection.

This is great news for those in ministry. Just as we feel an affinity with Christ the Enabler, so let us experience an affinity with Christ the Seeker. We don't always have to stand before our people as those who "have arrived," who know all the answers, for whom the questioning and searching are over. Let us attempt to emulate his life of seeking. Let us have the courage to think new thoughts in this time of change.

Encounter Time Bombs

With the shift from external to internal appropriation of faith, there must be a corresponding shift from pep talk ministry to encounter time bomb ministry. In the past, servants of the gospel were expected to master several versions of the pep talk. People came to us, we wound up the keys in their backs, and with luck they might keep going until the following Sunday. If they did, it was gratifying for us because we could see the immediate fruits of our ministerial endeavors. But the results tended to be short-lived. Pep-talk ministry, when done in isolation, does not contribute a great deal to internal appropriation of faith. It will always have its place, of course, but the changing times require what we call a time-bomb approach. Here the results are usually not immediate but go deeper and last longer.

In this kind of ministry, people are genuinely changed by the gospel message they hear, but the change is not perceptible right away. They may come from a prayer group or a liturgical celebration or a sermon or even a retreat, and feel that nothing significant has happened. Ask them at that moment what they got out of it, and in all honesty they answer, "nothing." They don't *feel* any different, so they presume that they aren't any different. But a few days or a week or even much later, they have an experience that surprises them. Perhaps in meeting a challenge they show unaccustomed courage. Or a cross is laid on them, and they are surprised at their ability to carry it. Or an unforeseen opportunity to serve may come their way, and they respond with a generosity they didn't know they had. What they didn't know was that an encounter time bomb was ticking in their heart, and only now does the actual love encounter take place. The timing of such encounters, of course, would depend not only on the human spirit but on the Holy Spirit.

The Christian Discovery Process is primarily an encounter time bomb ministry. Encounters may not be immediate, and they cannot be programmed. But when they do come, they are powerful and longlived. This book itself can be an occasion for such time bombs. They may be intellectual, leading to deeper insights into theology and ministry. More importantly, they may be encounter time bombs leading to new and deeper meetings with Christ and others.

In-Love / Out-Love

Why do you do ministry? To contribute to the increase of love within the communities you serve: school, parish, campus, religious group, diocese, nation. But there is a paradox here. Often the in-love of a group will grow just so much and then hit a ceiling. There it stays despite all your ministerial efforts. What to do? Answer: out-love. The people in the group have to get out of themselves, escape their own boundaries and widen the circle of concern. In doing so, they will find to their surprise that the group's in-love has grown of itself. This, in turn, will enable them to do more out-love . . . and so the spiral continually ascends.

There are many types of out-love in the world but one in particular cries out today for fulfillment. It goes by many names: justice and peace, social justice, Third World awareness, human rights. As the needy, the victimized, and the oppressed of the world become an integral part of the life of your community, so will that community's in-love grow. As "out there" becomes "in here" for your people, so will they begin to come alive. Practice out-love, and in-love will grow by leaps and bounds.

Step Ten

And so the Christian Discovery Process culminates in Step Ten. It goes by many names — fullness of Christian existence, fullness of space-time, Omega, the climax of creation-incarnation-salvation, the fullness of the Kingdom of God — whatever name is most meaningful for you. Remembering that we are dealing with the Unknown, the area of conjecture and hope, let us try for a vision, however speculative, of where Christian discovery is supposed to lead. Even a glimpse of our destination may illuminate the path upon which we journey and may even help us get there.

Omega-Kingdom is you in a resurrected state. It is the entire universe marvelously transformed to be the abode of your risen body. These two pieces of ultimate good news, your resurrection and the transformation of the universe, now come together. The entire universe becomes your resurrected body. It becomes the resurrected body of each of us. Limitations of space and time disappear in the fullness of life.

The implications are staggering. The entire universe now becomes Christ's resurrected body. It is the ultimate Eucharistic event. We are familiar with the Eucharist as memorial, which means more than just a remembering of past events as we do each year on the Fourth of July. Eucharist as memorial is an actual contact-communion, an experiencing of those events.

But the Eucharist is more than memorial; it is prophecy as well. Here is a prophetic foretaste of the ultimate reality that awaits us beyond the barriers of space and time. Now a piece of bread, a small amount of creation upon the altar, becomes Christ's resurrected body in a veiled manner. In the ultimate reality of Omega-Kingdom, the entire universe will become his risen body in an unveiled manner. You and Christ will enfold and embrace each other with the entire universe; you will completely compenetrate each other. And this same thing will happen among you and all others: the ultimate cherishing, the ultimate embrace.

There is a great paradox here. This ultimate embracing and enfolding, this ultimate union, will not diminish your own particular personality. In fact, it will be just the opposite: you will become *more you*. When the ultimate enhances your personality, you will become the total person truly alive that you are meant to be. As it is now, so even more will it be then: the greater your love, the more you grow as a person. Ultimate intimacy begets ultimate uniqueness.

And so the highest goal of all life, love and mysticism, will be attained: a universe totally alive, ultimate personality experiencing ultimate union with the beloved. This, then, is what Christ has won for us; this is what awaits us. And never forget: an unbelievable foretaste is possible in the here and now.

*   *   *

And that's the good news about the Good News!

---

[1]Briggs, K., "Religious Feeling Seen Strong in U.S.," *New York Times,* Dec. 9, 1984, p. 30.

[2]Ibid.

APPENDIX

THE ROLE OF THE RCIA*
IN THE PARISH

The church in the United States is fast becoming a mission church, and unless it adopts mission tactics, the church will lose the game of ministry.

Item: Father Philip Murnion, priest-sociologist of the New York archdiocese, in surveying religious attitudes of Catholics in the Yorkville section of Manhattan, found that among Catholics who no longer attended Mass, a startling 41 per cent did not believe in a personal God.

Item: In the United States there are some 12 million alienated Catholics. Moreover, sociologists tell us that another 68 million Americans are unchurched — that is, not affiliated with any church.

So to reach these 80 million Americans, the church must gradually transform the 18,000 parishes in the U.S. into mini-mission-sending societies.

The vision is grand, the challenge is great, and enthusiasm runs high. But the task is more easily stated than performed. Parish teams throughout the country must quickly realize that an in-depth preparation of parish members at large is needed if this outreach is to be accomplished successfully.

How is this preparation to be done? Mere exhortation by the parish teams and goodwill on the part of the members of the parishes will not suffice. There has to be a well-defined process of preparation for evangelization outreach. Is there an outline for such a preparatory process? Yes. It is the new Rite of Christian Initiation for Adults.

Most people view this rite as a process to be used exclusively for those who wish to join the church. "Of course it doesn't apply to us. We are born members of the church and, as such, above all this." There is a faint hint of the Pharisee praying in the Temple, "O God, I thank you that I am not like the rest of men." We would propose that the *entire parish* go through the process outlined in the rite. In short, each parish has to go through an evangelization process itself if it is to do successful evangelization outreach.

Although the documents on the rite speak of precatechumenate, catechumenate and so on, the entire process is an evangelization process. The documents on the new Rite provide us with an outline — the skeleton, if you will. What is needed now is a substance to flesh this out. The Christian Discovery Process consists of a series of search and encounter experiences. There is a great deal of content in the process, but it is no mere study course. It rests upon a strong experiential base. Let us now briefly consider how this process unfolds in conjunction with the outline of the new rite.

Precatechumenate. The surfacing and expanding of the person's basic heart wishes are probed — what ultimately one wants out of existence. The operative word is "expanding," for it is only in the expansion of basic heart wishes that one realizes the impossibility of attaining them by self alone. Only by deep love encounters with God and others can expanded basic heart wishes be fulfilled.

This process is followed by an experiential investigation of the dynamics and problems of encountering God and others.

The game can be won or lost at this primary level. Parish ministers are often so eager to share Scripture, Christ and church with parish members that they neglect this phase. They are then chagrined to see their ministerial efforts crumble for lack of a foundation.

Catechumenate. As the person attempts to encounter God and others, he or she soon realizes that this can't be done through one's own capacity alone. And so a primal cry goes forth from the person to God. Only with God's help will these encounter attempts ever attain their full potential and be truly successful.

God's response to this primal cry for help is an unfolding one. Scripture provides the initial response, but it is not so much Scripture as traditionally used in Cultural Christianity: a source of religious information. Rather, it is Scripture as encounter-causer. By this scriptural experience one comes to meet the God who has entered the human condition. Christ comes among us as *the* Encounter-Causer: to encounter you personally and to enable you to encounter others. Christ's life culminates in the Easter-Pentecost event, which is not just an event of 2,000 years ago but a process — a process by which the world is gradually swept up into encounter experience by the risen Christ. This ultimately is what church consists in. Primarily it is Easter-Pentecost process, and all organization, structure, distribution of power and such are answerable to this. The shift from static to dynamic concept of church has begun.

Purification and Enlightenment. Within church as Easter-Pentecost process, the risen Christ is particularly operative in encounters called sacraments. In light of all that has gone on before, the sacraments cease to be mere religious rituals to become love encounters with God and others brought about by Christ the Encounter-Causer.

Mystagogia. This is a time of reinforcement of previous aspects of the process: the principles by which the person can use Scripture as encounter-causer, and the dynamics of church as Easter-Pentecost process.

As the parish goes through the process, parish renewal results and with it a much deeper sense of community among members. As the awareness of community grows the need for smaller, more intimate groups will become apparent. Perhaps the future parish will consist of a series of small communities all sharing the physical plant of the parish. We see this already successfully working in the *communidades de base* — basic Christian communities — of Latin America.

The parish team often feels it is subject to a tidal wave of directives, exhortations, and requests from the bishops of the U.S. Yet all of these can be reduced to three themes: evangelization, parish renewal, and family. We have seen how preparation for evangelization outreach incorporates parish renewal. The two become one.

As for families, one of the biggest problems facing them has been the lack of communication between parents and children — particularly older adolescents — as they operate from different religious mindsets. If they had shared experience of the evangelization process discussed here, a true commonality would have been established — something that has been missing since the mid-sixties.

So you see, there exists the exciting possibility of all three ministerial objectives being encompassed in a single evangelization thrust.

----
* Rite of Christian Initiation of Adults.

3286